MASTERPIECE

MASTERPIECE

A MONTH OF MASTERPIECE MOMENTS

Carol Callahan

XULON PRESS

Xulon Press
555 Winderley Pl, Suite 225
Maitland, FL 32751
407.339.4217
www.xulonpress.com

© 2024 by Carol Callahan

All rights reserved solely by the author. The author guarantees all contents are original and do not infringe upon the legal rights of any other person or work. No part of this book may be reproduced in any form without the permission of the author.

Due to the changing nature of the Internet, if there are any web addresses, links, or URLs included in this manuscript, these may have been altered and may no longer be accessible. The views and opinions shared in this book belong solely to the author and do not necessarily reflect those of the publisher. The publisher therefore disclaims responsibility for the views or opinions expressed within the work.

Unless otherwise indicated, Scripture taken from The Passion Translation (TPT). Copyright © 2017 by Passion & Fire Ministries, Inc. Used by permission. All rights reserved. thePassionTranslation.com

Scripture quotations taken from the King James Version (KJV) – public domain.

Scripture quotations taken from the New King James Version (NKJV). Copyright © 1982 by Thomas Nelson, Inc. Used by permission. All rights reserved.

Scripture quotations taken from the Amplified Bible Classic Edition (AMPC). Copyright © 1954, 1958, 1962, 1964, 1965, 1987 by The Lockman Foundation. All rights reserved.

Scripture quotations taken from the Holy Bible, New International Version (NIV). Copyright © 1973, 1978, 1984, 2011 by Biblica, Inc.™. Used by permission. All rights reserved.

Scripture quotations taken from the Holy Bible, New Living Translation (NLT). Copyright ©1996, 2004, 2007 by Tyndale House Foundation. Used by permission of Tyndale House Publishers, Inc.

Scripture quotations taken from the English Standard Version (ESV). Copyright © 2001 by Crossway, a publishing ministry of Good News Publishers. Used by permission. All rights reserved.

Paperback ISBN-13: 979-8-86850-060-2
Ebook ISBN-13: 979-8-86850-061-9

DEDICATION

To Mom and Dad
who believed in me, encouraged me and whose influence,
even long after they moved to heaven, continues to motivate
me to always live for Jesus and to do my best.

To my husband, Denver,
Whose loving encouragement and incredible
patience have made this book possible.

To each person who reads this book and grants me
the privilege of being a participant in your journey to
the destiny God has for you, His masterpiece.

TABLE OF CONTENTS

Day 1	Handmade by the Master Creator	1
Day 2	A Poem in Process	5
Day 3	From one treasure to Another	9
Day 4	Discovering your Provenance	13
Day 5	A Princess in a Pigpen	17
Day 6	No Microwave Masterpieces	19
Day 7	Chosen To Be, Not Because	23
Day 8	Seeing the Unseen	27
Day 9	She Wore Blue Velvet	31
Day 10	Immanuel: When You Care Enough to Send the Very Best	35
Day 11	An Attitude Adjustment	39
Day 12	Distracted by the Master	43
Day 13	Born to Serve the Lord	47
Day 14	Never and Now	51
Day 15	When the Master Speaks	55
Day 16	Masterpiece in Motion	59

Day 17	Jesus the Master Influencer	63
Day 18	Messes Can Be Masterpieces	67
Day 19	With This Ring	71
Day 20	I've Been Framed!	75
Day 21	Shaped by the Master	79
Day 22	The Old Chimney	83
Day 23	Masterpieces Imagine	87
Day 24	Masterpieces Invest Wisely	91
Day 25	You're a Jewel	95
Day 26	Masterpieces Don't Need Masks	99
Day 27	You Want Me to Do What?	103
Day 28	Time…Not God's Problem	107
Day 29	A Walk with the Master	111
Day 30	Come Linger Longer	115
Day 31	Wrapped Up	119

FOREWORD

James 1:17 (NASB) tells us, "Every good thing given and every perfect gift is from above, coming down from the Father of lights, with whom there is no variation or shifting shadow." I can testify that God put Carol Callahan in my life as a good and perfect gift all wrapped up in one amazing woman. She is my wife and my partner in ministry. I can say from daily experience that she lives her life with a passionate love for God, her family, and for the people she meets.

Carol is laser focused on fulfilling God's plan for her purpose in the Kingdom of God and helping others to find theirs. As we have ministered side by side, I have observed up close her dedication to helping others discover how God sees them and how to live in that relationship. I have repeatedly heard testimonies of people who through Carol's ministry, written and spoken, have received the revelation, in spite of the circumstances life has thrown at them, that they are intricately and wonderfully created by God... a poem from his heart: They are God's masterpiece.

Masterpiece is a devotional book originally written for women, but its message applies to men as well. Its purpose is to encourage, build confidence, and increase every reader's faith in the truth that God created us and we are all His masterpiece.

As you read each day's devotion, you will become aware of the anointing of the Holy Spirit on Carol as she shares the revelation she has received as she wrote these pages. With great transparency, often from personal experience, she reveals the powerful truth that your past experiences, circumstances, even your failures, are not your identity. They are not how God sees you. Regardless of your situation, there is freedom and joy in being able to look in the mirror and say to that person looking back at you, "You do not define me. God does. I am a masterpiece."

1 Peter 5:8 (NASB) says: "Your adversary, the devil, prowls around like a roaring lion, seeking someone to devour." John 10:10 (NASB) explains further: "he comes to steal, to kill, and destroy." That is why you will find Carol's message in this book invaluable. She reveals how the enemy distorts our true identity through causing us to see life's situations and circumstances through the filter of his lies. Carol unapologetically and unrelentingly exposes that lie and encourages the reader to discover and live in your true identity as God's masterpiece, created in His image, perhaps not perfect, but perfectly loved and in the process of being shaped by the Master.

Carol is a published author and public speaker; women of all ages and from all walks of life have experienced the life-changing love of God through her open-hearted, personally caring writing style. I endorse, without hesitation, *Masterpiece: A Month of Masterpiece Moments*. I recommend and encourage you to experience the anointing that flows through this gift that I call my wife, Carol Callahan, lover of God and of His people.

Denver Callahan
Pastor, Lifelines Church
Springfield, Missouri

INTRODUCTION

A few years ago, my husband, Denver, and I moved into a new home. We were welcomed by several of our neighbors during the first few weeks we lived here…most of them bringing a plate of goodies along with a welcoming smile. One couple brought over a plate of still-warm cookies; in conversation we discovered they are Christians, too.

We told them we are pastors and began sharing our heart for ministry, including how excited I was about the women's conference I was planning. She jumped into the conversation quickly with, "I've gone to a few women's conferences because I was singing at them, but I really don't like them. They all insist on telling me I'm beautiful. I know I'm not! And I refuse to let someone make me say I am." Frankly, I was stunned and not quite sure how to respond.

They are wonderful neighbors. She has surprised us with pots of yummy soup, fresh-out-of-the-oven homemade bread, and a variety of cookies. Her warm, caring spirit is more beautiful to me than the face of any famous model. She IS beautiful because she is exactly what God created her to be…a masterpiece! But she doesn't believe it.

That experience fueled my passion to see myself as God sees me and to help others see themselves that way, too. It isn't always easy to overcome a poor self-image and to see myself as God does. We all see the ads, watch the TV shows, and read the stories about beautiful, perfectly proportioned, well-dressed, women with perfect, white smiles. Our emotional response to what we see (or don't see) in the mirror can completely drown out the voice of the Spirit. He reminds us He lives in us and that our identity is in Christ, not in others' opinions. We are, after all, created in His image.

Admit it. What the world tells you about yourself and how it defines a masterpiece can totally block any other message—for instance, God saying you are *fearfully and wonderfully made* (Ps 139:14 KJV).

Anything you do consistently over time becomes a habit. My prayer is that after 31 days of experiencing masterpiece moments through the pages of this book the reader will have developed the habit of believing its message: You are God's masterpiece!

DAY 1
HANDMADE BY THE MASTER CREATOR

*For we are God's masterpiece (*Ep 2:10 NLT*).*

A masterpiece is a work of artistry that demonstrates skill or workmanship. Its identity is determined not by its own nature, but by the skill and ability of the one who created it. This shifts the focus from the object to the master. Therefore, our status as masterpieces is 100% dependent on God's artistry, skill, and workmanship, not on anything we do, think, or achieve. We don't make ourselves a masterpiece…God does!

Some translations use the word "handiwork" rather than "masterpiece" in Ephesians 2:10. That translation emphasizes an important truth: masterpieces are hand-created. We are handmade by *the* Creator. That is the essential difference between us and the rest of creation. God said, *Let there be light…let there be a firmament…let the waters under the heavens be gathered together into one place and let the dry land appear…let the earth bring forth grass, the herb that yields seed according to its kind, and the tree that yields fruit…let there be lights in the firmament of the heavens…let the waters abound with an abundance of living creatures and let birds fly above the earth…let the earth bring forth the living creature according to its kind* (Ge 1:3-25 NKJV). But then He changed His process. He said, *"Let Us make man in our image, according to our likeness…* (verse 26 NKJV). Out of all His creation, we are His only handmade masterpiece. We are the only one He personally shaped in His own image and into whom He breathed His own breath, the breath of life.

Even after man sinned, God's plan remained unchanged: to be in relationship with the ones He "made in His image." How was that to be possible? Jesus would come to earth, live, and die as a man; He would pay the price on the cross for sin, and rise again to restore the unique relationship of the Creator with His masterpiece.

On your worst days, this is your hope. On your best days, it is your joy. From your first to your last breath here on earth, you are in the masterpiece process. That should comfort and encourage you! When you find yourself questioning your abilities, value, or accomplishments, you can rely on your masterpiece status. You are a handmade sign of God's creativity, power, and loving connection with man. And that is just the way He planned it!

We are assured of how He feels about us in Psalm 100:3 where it says: *And realize what this really means—we have the privilege of worshiping Yahweh our God. For he is our Creator, and we belong to him. We are the people of his pleasure* (TPT).

He is our Creator, and we belong to Him; we are His pleasure. Imagine that! Despite all our flaws and imperfections, we are privileged to worship Him, belong to Him, and bring Him pleasure! You can choose to be defined by the standards of this world, or you can find your identity in your relationship with your Creator. The moment you recognize and claim your masterpiece status—a handmade, loved, and treasured creation of God himself—what others think is unimportant. God chooses to sign His name on you, not only proclaiming His ownership, but also His delight in what He has created. Amazing!

I remember when, as a student/writer, the first manuscript I ever submitted for publication was accepted. I was so excited to see my masterpiece in print! (I think I received an impressive $17 for it.) But when my copy arrived in the mail, I was crushed. It was my article, but with a new title and edited to half its original length. To me it was barely recognizable as my creation.

But I learned an important lesson. I submitted a good article, but skilled editors had improved it. It was still mine. It still conveyed my message. And, for this aspiring writer, the best thing was unchanged: My name was still on it. I was a published writer! I clipped that article and started a collection of my "masterpieces" in print.

There is a powerful connection between master and masterpiece… between The Master and His masterpieces. He cares about our process. He cares about all the things we go through, all the edits made by life. Because He cares, we are not defined by the journey from mess to masterpiece. Instead, He consistently sees us as He created us to be. He never focuses on our past; He continues to identify us as His masterpiece…a creation, possibly still in process, but one He loves and claims as His own.

My memories from today's moments with the Master…

_____

_____

_____

Conversation with the Master…

God, thank You for making me a handcrafted masterpiece. With absolute trust, I put myself in Your hands knowing You love me, have a destiny for me, and will continue shaping my life into the masterpiece You planned for me to be from the beginning of time.

DAY 2
A POEM IN PROCESS

We have become his poetry... (Ep 2:10 TPT).

I love to "people-watch!" Airports and malls are prime viewing arenas. And don't even get me started on Walmart shoppers! I try not to be rude and stare, but I find it fascinating to observe God's masterpieces-in-process. People are funny...people are sad...they come in all shapes, sizes, and personalities. And God created them all—one Creator, infinite variety!

You see, each masterpiece is unique. There is an infinite variety of masterpieces. You can find them in theaters or museums, on easels or pottery wheels, on public display or in a private collection. Some are to be read, some to be viewed, some to be experienced. The one thing they have in common is a creative process that reveals something of their creator.

During my people-watching, I've decided some reveal God's sense of humor (I find a lot of those in Walmart!). There is nearly poetic beauty in more personal moments, for example, at the bedside of a dying loved one, or in a dimly lit nursery where a mother soothes her feverish child. Wherever they are found, they reflect the Master's creative nature. They are His original, living poetry.

When you study Ephesians 2:10 in various Bible translations, you find different words used for "masterpiece"—for example, handiwork, workmanship, creation, and poetry. I like the translation "poetry" used by The Passion Translation in this verse. It comes from the Greek word "poiema," which is the root for the English words "poem" and "poetry." Our new life in Christ is a new, supernatural work of divine poetry. We are, in essence, His poetic masterpieces!

Poetry isn't our typical form of expression in daily conversation. Creating a poem involves conscious thought, effort, and skill. Making use of form, meter, patterns, careful word choices, and imagination, a poet creates images for our minds. Poems, like God's creation of man, are neither accidental nor haphazard and their value may not be apparent on first reading. However, whether we initially understand the value or meaning of the poem or not, the poet's plan remains. In the heart of the Creator the plan for you, the plan for me, remains unchanged and has since before the foundation of the earth. Imagine! You are a perfect expression of God's creative plan for you. And that plan hasn't changed from before time began.

One definition of "poem" is, "something that arouses strong emotions because of its beauty." ("poem"; *www.dictionary.com*) If you are like me, you have difficulty wrapping your mind around the description of yourself as being beautiful—something that arouses strong emotions. I find myself thinking, "You've got to be kidding! Me? **I arouse strong emotions because I'm so beautiful?"**

Yes, it's true. Because, you see, beauty isn't as much a matter of appearance as it is of fulfilling your destiny…being what God created you to be and seeing yourself that way. God absolutely delights in you! He loves you; He sees you as beautiful. You are evidence that His plan is working!

In the moments when we perceive ourselves as anything but a creative, poetic masterpiece, we need a spiritual eye exam. We need to see as God sees. How did Jesus see them when He was selecting His disciples? His perception of their qualifications and abilities clearly didn't match how others saw them, or even how they saw themselves. Someone once aptly described the disciples this way:

- Simon Peter—emotionally unstable and given to fits of anger

- Andrew—absolutely no qualities of leadership
- James and John—place personal interests above company loyalty
- Thomas—demonstrates a questioning attitude in a way that would tend to undermine morale
- Matthew—has been blacklisted by the Jerusalem Better Business Bureau
- James and Thaddeus—definitely have radical leanings and demonstrate manic/depressive tendencies
- Judas—great potential, ability, and resourcefulness, meets people well, keen business mind, contacts in high places, motivated and ambitious

And yet Jesus chose them all! He saw them for what He would make of them–according to His plan, not as they appeared in that moment.

If Jesus were selecting disciples today, He would certainly view you and me very differently than others do. He sees us as He designed us to be. He envisions the poem, the beauty wrapped in human form. Believing in the poetic beauty He wrote into our life stories before we were even born, He continues to develop us according to His original plan.

See yourself as God saw Jeremiah: *Before I formed you in the womb I knew [and] approved of you [as my chosen instrument], and before you were born I separated and set you apart, consecrating you...* (Je 1:5 <u>AMP</u>).

You are daily developing into the poetic masterpiece God wrote when He designed your life long before you were even born, and despite what you may or may not believe about yourself. If it helps develop your ability to see yourself this way, each morning look at yourself in the mirror and declare: "I am God's poem and He approves of me."

My memories from today's moments with the Master...

_____

_____

_____

Conversation with the Master...

Thank you, Master, for the promise that I am created and loved by You, and that You see me as Your masterpiece. Please give me a spiritual eye exam and correct my vision so that I see myself as You see me...as Your poetic masterpiece, a skillfully crafted and chosen instrument.

DAY 3
FROM ONE TREASURE TO ANOTHER

For we are God's masterpiece. He has created us anew in Christ Jesus so we can do the good things he planned for us long ago (Eph 2:10 NLT).

There are days when I get up in the morning, look in the mirror, and see anything but a masterpiece. At times throughout the day when I walk by a mirror, I'm tempted to wonder what anyone, let alone God, sees in me. There are even days that I end up back at the mirror washing my face and wishing I could wash away the image I see there. I'm sure I'm not unique in that. We can all be hard on ourselves, in fact, our own greatest critic.

Though people may be more than willing to say things that cause us to see ourselves as losers–as less or a mess–do you realize God never sees or describes you that way? Never. Not ever. Not for a minute! Never has. Never will. He **always** sees you as His personal, handcrafted creation. And He has big plans for that creation, plans He made "long ago" according to Ephesians 2:10.

That message is not Paul's alone, though. Our Father, the Master, wants you to know this is His message for you and me today—in fact, every day. While you're reading this page He is watching and wanting you to hear Him: "You are My masterpiece; you please Me."

Do you find yourself doubting that declaration? You're in good company. I'm positive Apostle Peter felt like an ugly failure many times in his life, too. We know now how his story eventually turned out and what

God's plans for him turned out to be; however, the night Peter took a walk on the water and took a dip in the waves, he very likely did not see himself as a masterpiece…more like a sinking loser. Later, standing by a fire outside the gate where Jesus had been taken prisoner, he was no doubt horrified when he heard himself swearing that he didn't even know Jesus. As he ran away weeping, He unquestionably felt more like a hot mess than a masterpiece.

But because Jesus is the Master, He made major modifications in Peter's life and to his view of himself. Peter later wrote: *But you are God's chosen treasure…He called you out of darkness to experience his marvelous light, and now he claims you as his very own* (1Pe 2:9 TPT).

Peter finally got it! He wrote to us as one treasure—one masterpiece—to another. He experienced the feeling of being in the dark where it was impossible to see clearly. But he also knew what it was to be called into the light where His identity in Christ was revealed. He learned from experience that even failures, when reshaped by the hand of the Master, can become masterpieces.

Jesus claims us as His own and, as masters do with their treasured creations, He certifies the authenticity of the masterpiece by signing it. By inscribing His name on us, He proclaims to the world that we are His valued handiwork. *He did this so that you would broadcast his glorious wonders throughout the world* (1Pe 2:9 TPT).

He planned for you, his sometimes-messy masterpiece, to be His best advertisement. No matter how bad things look in the make-up mirror, God lovingly reshapes us into what He created us to be…revealing His image in and through us. The process may have to be repeated and our image constantly refined, but through each step of the process, we are His living creation, His handiwork, His poetry in motion. Continually, He leads us toward a destiny fit for a one-of-a-kind masterpiece.

Today you may not be feeling it. In fact, you may feel like a failure and as if your life is a disappointment to everyone, including God. You may believe you have ruined His plan for you. Not true! You do not have the power to do that. Nothing you do, or don't do, destroys the plan God set in motion from the beginning. Because He is bigger than our failures, He consistently reminds us, "Stay in the journey; don't give up. The destiny I planned for you long, long ago is nearer than it has ever been. I'm delighted with you, my masterpiece—not just the way you are, but the way you are becoming as I hold and shape you in my hands.

From one treasure to another, may I tell you, we may not "have this," but God does. Every day. Every time. Always.

My memories from today's moments with the Master…

_____

_____

_____

Conversation with the Master…

Father, I see a very imperfect person when I look in the mirror. I identify with Peter in his weakness and failures. But now I choose to allow You, my Master, to replace the darkness of my self-criticism with Your marvelous light. Just as You did for Peter, lead me out of my mess and into Your masterpiece plan for me.

DAY 4
DISCOVERING YOUR PROVENANCE

Don't you realize that your body is the temple of the Holy Spirit, who lives in you and was given to you by God? You do not belong to yourself, for God bought you with a high price (1Co 6:19, 20 NLT).

Not every masterpiece is in a museum. In fact, they are not all anyplace you might expect. I enjoy stories about ordinary people who find and purchase unusual, or even ordinary-appearing, items at a yard sale only to discover they purchased for next to nothing a valuable treasure. We can all dream, right?

I've watched the discovery of amazingly valuable items on the program "Antiques Roadshow." It's enough to make a girl clean out the attic, the garage…maybe even Grandma's old stuff! People come to a Roadshow event carrying odd pieces of jewelry, paintings found in a pile of junk, items they can't even identify; experts examine the items, research if necessary, and assign an evaluation or price range. Amazingly, some true treasures are revealed.

For example, one young lady brought a ring to be examined. It had been her grandmother's. Eventually it was given to the current owner by her father to wear in her wedding as her "something blue." Its huge blue stone was surrounded by smaller diamonds. Twice in the past, she had taken the ring to jewelers to be appraised. It was never valued at more than $250. The owner decided it was worth one more try at the Antiques Roadshow.

After a very careful look, he gave the owner of the ring news that left her speechless. The huge blue stone was the largest and finest sapphire the man had ever personally seen (not glass as previous appraisals had claimed) and the stones around it were real and valuable diamonds (not worthless as appraised before) set in silver and mounted in gold. The ring was worth at least $35,000.

One of the clues the experts investigate in evaluating items is called "provenance." An item's provenance is "the record of ownership of a work of art or of an antique, used as a guide to authenticity or quality." ("provenance; *www.dictionary.com*) It adds value when an item's provenance is available and reveals a connection to a master artist or a significant history. The material, source, function, and condition matter—not necessarily individually, but taken together by someone who really knows the value each carries when combined with the others.

As God's masterpiece, your provenance is known and proves your incredible worth. *Know that the Lord is God. It is He who made us, and we are His* (Ps 100:3 NIV).

There is no better record of ownership. You are authentic and of the finest quality! The body of work of your Creator is priceless; each piece carries His signature clearly establishing provenance.

Thus says the Lord, your Redeemer, and He Who formed you from the womb: I am the Lord who made all things, Who alone stretched out the heavens, Who spread out the earth by Myself" (Is 44:24 AMPC).

On days when Satan tries to make you feel worthless, ugly, forsaken, or useless, you can remind him of your provenance. You were created in—handmade and fashioned to bear—God's image. And, incidentally, He created everything else, too. He has an impeccable reputation. But the best part is you are not only His look-alike creation, but you were also purposely designed to bring Him glory. You weren't intended to be displayed in a museum, but to live in His presence as His treasured child. When sin tried to steal your value, Jesus came to earth to redeem you. To what the world saw as worthless, Jesus assigned infinite worth and He paid with His own blood to redeem you.

Discovering Your Provenance

You are authentic. You are first quality. You are God's masterpiece.

My memories from today's moments with the Master…

_____

_____

_____

Conversation with the Master…

Lord, I thank you that I know where I came from…my provenance. You not only formed my body in my mother's womb, but You continue to shape me into your image. I am a valuable masterpiece because Your Son, Jesus, redeemed me. I know I am never worthless, lost, or second rate. I am authentic, first quality, and valued by You, the Master.

DAY 5
A PRINCESS IN A PIGPEN

But you are a chosen generation, a royal priesthood, an holy nation, a peculiar people (1Pe 2:9 KJV).

I have spent an exorbitant amount of time in my life conforming to people's expectations of me and losing my God-given identity in the process. The world will, in its most religious-sounding voice, say that adapting, going along to get along, is the loving, even Christian, thing to do. They lie!

Fitting in becomes pretending; and pretending generally deceives only the pretender. God created every one of us for a purpose. We fulfill that purpose only when we find our identity in living life according to His plan, His way. I've discovered that fitting into a space you're not designed to fill eventually fails. Solomon gave good advice for making better choices: *Trust in the Lord completely, and do not rely on your own opinions. With all your heart rely on Him to guide you, and he will lead you in every decision you make"* (Pr 3:5 TPT).

Purpose is found in trusting God's plan, while pigpens are located in the pit of personal opinions. For example, everyone knows the story of the Prodigal son. His opinion of his father's plan for him led him quickly from home to hopeless. His escape from his father's "control" masqueraded as freedom—for a while. But when the money and the dream ran out, he was left in a place no prince would choose—the pigpen. Dreams die in pigpens of disobedience.

Masterpiece

You weren't created for life in a pigpen of failure. In 1 Peter 2:9, Peter reminds us of our identity: a chosen generation…a royal priesthood…God's favored child. It is impossible to live well where you don't belong. Imagine an eagle choosing to live in a birdcage designed for a hummingbird…or a hummingbird trying to live the life of an eagle. Both are beautiful birds, but neither is safe nor satisfied in the other's world. They must live where God designed them to flourish.

You will never fulfill your created purpose as God's masterpiece if you do not trust His plan. Birds can't live in fishbowls and fish can't fly. We all need to live the life for which the Master designed us. The moral of the story? Never be satisfied to be a princess/prince in a pigpen!

My memories from today's moments with the Master…

_____

_____

_____

Conversation with the Master…

> *Because of You, Lord, I am not a princess in a pigpen. I'm not an eagle in a birdcage. I am everything You created me to be! I trust You to be my guide in every choice I make and every path I follow. I rely on You to direct me to the goal for which You have chosen me: to be Your masterpiece.*

DAY 6
NO MICROWAVE MASTERPIECES

When it seems as though you are facing nothing but difficulties, see it as an invaluable opportunity to experience the greatest joy that you can! it will release perfection into every part of your being until there is nothing missing and nothing lacking." (Ja 1:2, 4b <u>TPT</u>).

Given the choice, most of us would prefer the simple, speedy microwave version of our development into a masterpiece. But the process usually more closely resembles microwave popcorn…everything that will be evident in the finished product is hidden in the tough, little kernel. Its explosive potential is not revealed until it experiences the heat. We want to be a big, fluffy, yummy bite of deliciousness; instead, in the beginning, we are kernels that hold the promise, but look nothing like the anticipated final product.

Moving from basic ingredients to culinary masterpiece in two or three easy steps and five minutes fits our American lifestyle—the less time and effort required the better. It's perfectly acceptable to sacrifice quality and flavor for quick and filling. But God isn't limited or constrained by time. So, while our microwave culture is focused on fast and easy, He is working outside of time and recognizes none of its limitations and constraints. The idea of removing time from the equation of life is nearly impossible for us to conceive. We become frustrated when forced to wait. We see patience as a problem, not a virtue. But our Master Creator is more concerned with the final product over the process and with destiny over schedules.

Excruciatingly, we must listen and obey when He says, *Be still and know that I am God* (Ps 46:10 NIV).

Culinary masterpieces rarely result from microwave recipes; God's masterpieces seldom develop according to our desire for quick and easy. Instead, they are a combination of quality ingredients, thoughtful preparation, concentrated effort, a big portion of love, and time to perfect the details. Simple, quick, and easy happens, but rarely.

I am known to start big projects expecting exciting outcomes only to discover the process is way more difficult than I expected. I hit one roadblock after another. I learn. I stretch my limits. Sometimes I'm tempted to give up. But then, as I conquer one step after another, purely by determination, I begin to feel the joy in overcoming obstacles and in winning. The battle to reach each succeeding step becomes motivation to continue moving forward and to celebrate each victory along the way.

We can learn to have joy in the journey (even with its detours and delays), celebration in the victories (even the small ones), and peace in the process (even when it's painful). This makes me think of God's people transforming what should have been an 11-day trip into 40 years of wandering. This was definitely **not** what they thought they had signed up for! From the first day after their great escape, they faced situations that were much more than "difficult." They lived with heat, dust, and whiney traveling companions. There was no water, bitter water, no food and an unchanging diet of manna. It was not a vacation!

Finally, they were close enough to look across into their promised land. And there they saw giants! Huge guys. Guys who saw them as grasshoppers according to most of the spies sent in to scope out the situation. This did not match their expectations. They were God's people, after all! They deserved better. The challenge defeated them before their enemies could.

I can identify. Sometimes my hopes and dreams seem to turn into nightmares. I work and work and save and save, and just when I have enough money to go on that dream vacation, a storm hits, and the vacation fund goes for home repairs. Here's the lesson I have learned: I can celebrate having a home to repair. Many people don't. I am blessed to be able to earn and save allowing me to dream; some people have little to nothing fueling hope in their life.

And so, I find joy in my journey. I realize each blessing in my life is a gift to be celebrated. And before long, the celebration shuts down my pity party. I can be thankful. Joy releases peace and perfection—nothing missing and nothing lacking.

Be encouraged. No matter how difficult the path ahead looks, tackle the hard stuff. Allow it to develop your inner joy. Then live with "nothing missing and nothing lacking"—the true meaning of peace.

Pursue peace in your journey. It doesn't come out of a microwave, but it's incredibly enjoyable and satisfying.

My memories from today's moments with the Master…

_____

_____

_____

Conversation with the Master…

Your word tells us to be still and know that You are God. I admit that being still and waiting doesn't come naturally. So, I need Your supernatural presence in my process. I will not expect masterpiece results from a microwave effort. I am expecting Your peace and joy as I allow You to set the pace of my journey.

DAY 7
CHOSEN TO BE, NOT BECAUSE

"I was chosen by God to be…" (Eph 1:1 TPT).

When I married my husband, one of the most difficult things for me to learn was to trust him— to believe he accepted and valued me as a gift from God, not for anything I did or had. The confidence necessary to enter marriage grew only from realizing God had chosen us for one another. We were both broken by past experiences and were determined to protect ourselves from a reoccurrence. And then, the first time we ever met in person, God told us His plan: "This is going to be your spouse." He chose us to be someone and something neither of us ever expected to be or to have.

It was clear to both of us that this had to be God's choice. Nothing we had ever done qualified us for a second chance, let alone a new beginning in a blessed marriage. On my own I could never have been what Denver needed; and he knew his qualification to be the husband I needed was purely in his obedience to God. He chose us **to be.** For our wedding, Denver wrote a song called "For Heaven's Sake." Years later, we are still living as man and wife "for heaven's sake" …because that is His design and plan for us.

God's choices are always revealed through a process and for a purpose. In Ephesians 1:1 Paul identifies himself by both. He was chosen for the purpose of being. For him it was to be an apostle of Jesus. He was chosen **to be** not because of how he saw himself, but because of God's plan for him. Paul could never have imagined himself in that relationship—in fact, before he met Jesus on the road to Damascus, he was running hard in the opposite direction.

After Saul, as he was known then, picked himself up off the dirt road, his first question, found in Acts *9:5,* was, *"Who are you?"* After being knocked down, he could have demanded, "What are you doing?" But it was more important to know Who he was dealing with than to demand an explanation. Only after the Who was answered was there an answer to the what question: *"Lord, what do you want me to do" (*Ac 9:6 NKJV*)?* There is always a purpose in the plan. There was one for Saul/Paul; there is for you.

Do you realize that everything God has ever done here on earth has been to establish and maintain relationship with His masterpieces? With us? He knows everything about us and still chooses and uses us in His masterplan. David understood the pervasive power of that and describes it in Psalm 139:16, 17. Fellow masterpiece, as you read these words, hear the heart of God: *You saw who you created me to be before I became me! Before I'd ever seen the light of day, the number of days you planned for me were already recorded in your book. Every single moment you are thinking of me!* (TPT)

We are chosen to **be**, not to **do**. God thinks about us every moment because He knows who we are, not because of what we do. Other people might be able to do the same things, but each one of us has a one-of-a-kind relationship with our Creator—the One who chose us before we were even conceived!

When you feel confused, when you find yourself wondering who you are, remember: You are God's masterpiece. He thinks about you every single minute. He chose you. In your mother's womb He wove together all you would become. In a culture in which people are confused, unsure of their identity, longing to belong and to be accepted, the answer is the same for every person: You are chosen to be God's masterpiece and to be all He created for you to be. My name coming from His mouth is "Carol the Masterpiece." You can insert your name in that sentence!

We are chosen to be, not because.

My memories from today's moments with the Master…

_____

_____

_____

Conversation with the Master…

> *Sometimes I forget, God, that I can't earn Your love; You freely give it. You think about me every single moment! I find comfort and peace in knowing that all I must **be** is Yours. Help me to remember You don't need a "because" to love me,*

DAY 8
SEEING THE UNSEEN

God, all at once you turned on a floodlight for me! You are the revelation-light in my darkness, and in your brightness I can see the path ahead (Ps 18:28 TPT).

For several years we lived in "the country." We shared 40+ acres with an assortment of critters. I found possums eating out of the cat's food bowl on the front porch; raccoons made regular raids on our trash dumpster; owls peered in our skylights. My least favorite neighbors were the slithery ones who hid out under leaves, in trees, and by the lake. Just seeing snakes made my toes curl up and my heart pound. But my favorite animal sightings were of deer. I was never sure where or when they would appear, but I was on constant lookout.

That season of country living was not all about the animals, though. It was a difficult season for me. There were unexpected changes in our life, difficult relationships, financial setbacks, and tears…lots and lots of tears. I never stopped loving and trusting God; and I knew He loved me. I struggled, though, to feel His presence and personal involvement in my life as I had at other times. I couldn't see Him working anything, let alone "all things," for my good. Despite all I knew about God and all He had done in my life, I couldn't make this season work for me. I wondered, "Why has He put me here? Where is He in all the mess? What is He doing while I'm here hurting and confused?"

In the middle of my struggle, He sent me a personal message. I had been watching for deer as usual, but none had appeared for quite a while.

Then, one morning I glanced out the window overlooking our yard and lake and glimpsed movement over to one side. The biggest buck I had ever seen on the property came strolling across the yard. He took his time. I quietly moved to where I could see him more clearly. His antlers were impressive. But what I noticed was that he had several scars on his back and sides. Clearly, he had endured some painful experiences. He was magnificent but scarred. I was mesmerized by what I was seeing. Just a few yards from me, he was casually nibbling our grass, occasionally raising his head to check for danger, and then returning to his meal.

In that moment, I heard the Lord saying, "He's been out there all along. He was out of sight, but as real and nearly as close to you as he is right now. I've been with you all along, too. You don't see me, but I am close. Learn to trust me when you see no evidence. I'm near, always working in your life."

There may be seasons in the life of even a masterpiece when it's difficult to discern the presence of the Master. At those times He may be moving things all around you; without your awareness or permission, He transforms your life…in His time. The truth is that destiny is rarely revealed by circumstances.

Think about David when he was living in a cave accompanied by a ragtag group of society's misfits. (You can read the account of this in 1 Samuel 22 and 23.) Caves are not for kings. He would not stay there forever. And, as bad as his circumstances appeared at that moment, God was preparing him to be king—as impossible as that surely felt during the waiting. Remember, you may have to take up temporary residence in the cave of preparation or trial; if so, it may well be your pathway to the palace of your destiny.

In the Bible we aren't given a detailed story of the life of Rahab. But, like David, she found her way to masterpiece status despite her circumstances. In the beginning, not only did she not see God at work in her life, but she also didn't know Him; she knew only His reputation. She was aware that everyone in Jericho, a well-fortified city, was terrified by the arrival of the Jews in their area. She knew about the encampment of God's people nearby and probably assumed they were preparing to attack. However, she knew nothing of how this was going to change her life from mess (being a prostitute pretty much qualifies her for the label) to masterpiece…she was eventually in the lineage of David and of Jesus. She was transformed from prostitute to priceless treasure. In the process, she moved from living as a prostitute in her home on the wall of Jericho to living in a tent in the Hebrew camp as the wife of one of the spies she protected in her previous home. Did it look like her situation qualified her to be remembered in what we call the Hall of Faith in Hebrews 11? Not really. But *By faith the harlot Rahab perished not with them that believed not, when she had received the spies with peace* (He 11:31 KJV).

She trusted the God she could not see, did not know, and with whom she had no "history," and He worked all things around her for her good. We have the promise that the same God works the same way for us. We may not be able to discern what He is doing just beyond our view and ability to understand, but that does not change the truth that He is the Master of the masterpiece. That masterpiece is me. That masterpiece is you.

My memories from today's moments with the Master…

_____

_____

_____

Conversation with the Master…

Lord, I am learning to trust You even when I can't see You at work in my life. Teach me to recognize Your presence, even in the difficult times. I want to learn to discern Your presence and to trust Your invisible involvement. In my dark moments, I choose to allow Your revelation- light to brighten my path.

DAY 9
SHE WORE BLUE VELVET

The Lord delights in those who fear him, who put their hope in His unfailing love. (Ps 147:11 <u>NIV</u>).

Even masterpieces need to experience their own moment…you know, that instant when you feel loved, appreciated, and beautiful. I love it when a masterpiece moment plan comes together! But, for many women, if not most, those moments are rare. That makes the experience even more valuable.

One of my "moments" came very early in my life. It was the night I graduated from kindergarten. In honor of the momentous occasion, my mother had purchased a blue velvet dress for me to wear. It was beautiful—my version of Cinderella's ball gown. The afternoon of the big event Mama scrubbed my bruised and scabby legs and arms (that was the season of learning to ride my bike), shampooed my hair, and made sure it was silky soft by applying what we called "cream rinse" in those days. Not a speck of dirt nor a pesky tangle was going to detract from my blue velveted beauty!

According to my five-year-old memories, my entrance into the room in the church basement where we all gathered was breathtaking. I was sure all conversation stopped as I entered in all my scrubbed up, scabby glory. And, wonder of all wonders, the boy I had a huge, if secret, crush on came over and said I looked "very nice."

It was my moment. Nothing could spoil it. If I never had another one, it was magnificent! I treasure the memory of my blue velvet memory.

As the years have passed, I realize it was not wearing blue velvet that made me special that night. It was who I was inside the dress. I was aware for the first time in my life that God had made me special. You see, the truth is that I was the same Carol, in a scrubbed up and beautifully attired version, that I was every day in my plain school clothes, on my wobbly bike, or snuggled up on my Daddy's lap being comforted after a fall on my roller skates. Blue Velvet Carol had always been there. She is still in there. She's the masterpiece in the middle of the mess that is my routine most days…days when I feel not at all special, when my circumstances convince me I am not pretty at all, days when I'm ordinary.

Thinking about Blue Velvet Carol reminds me of Queen Esther. She was an orphaned Jewish girl living in Babylon as a captive. Being attractive and having character had limited value for an exile living under the rule of a king who valued only what pleased and made him look good. But then the Master's hand began working for His masterpiece Esther in a very unusual way. It was impossible that Esther could have guessed that what was going on in the royal citadel of Susa was about to change her life…and the lives of many more.

When she was chosen to go to the palace to be groomed for the king, she had no clue this was God's plan for saving the lives of His people. She did not anticipate a blue velvet experience. Dragged away from her home, forced to live surrounded by the wicked lifestyle of the palace, she was scrubbed, anointed, fixed up and trained…trained to please not a freckle-faced five-year-old kindergartner, but Nebuchadnezzar, King of Babylon.

> *She was taken to [the king] in the royal palace…the king fell in love with Esther…he was totally smitten by her. He placed a royal crown on her head and made her queen* (Es 2: 16-17 MSG).

There's so much more to the story, but the most important truth is that Esther was the same person in fine clothing and jewels and smelling of fine perfumes that she was every day before being taken to the palace.

It wasn't the king's attention and approval that gave her value, but the King of King's plan for her life.

In the moments when you feel valueless, hopeless, unattractive to anyone—and we all have them at some, maybe many, points of time—God sees you as His masterpiece. He sees you as He created you to be. And He loves you…just like that!

As intimidating as it may seem, God knows all about us, always has, always will. That is not a threat, but a promise: *Before I shaped you in the womb, I knew all about you. Before you saw the light of day, I had holy plans for you*" (Je 1:5 NIV).

Enjoy the promise of the plan. God knows what is ahead, and He says it is good: *"For I know the plans I have for you," declares the Lord, "plans to prosper you and not to harm you, plans to give you hope and a future"* (Je 29:11 NIV).

He sees you always in blue velvet!

> *…who knows whether you have come to the kingdom for such a time as this?* (Es 4:14 NKJV).

My memories from today's moments with the Master…

_____

_____

_____

Conversation with the Master…

> *Lord, You know that some days I feel totally unlovely. But I am thankful that You always see me as the person You designed me to be. Your unfailing love looks beyond my physical appearance and sees me as Your masterpiece in blue velvet (or blue jeans). I am, and will always be, all wrapped up in your love.*

DAY 10

IMMANUEL: WHEN YOU CARE ENOUGH TO SEND THE VERY BEST

*She will give birth to a son, and they will call him Immanuel, which means "God with us." (*Ma 1:23 <u>NLT</u>*)*.

My mother always chose the perfect card for every occasion and for every person. We all knew the process. She always shopped for her favorite brand—Hallmark. She apparently believed in caring "enough to send the very best." Not only was her source consistent, but also her method. She would stand at the card rack for long…oh, so long… periods of time reading every appropriate or possibly appropriate card available; then, very often, she would go back to the first or second one she had looked at and select it.

Mom's actions remind me a lot of how God does things, I think because she always taught me to make my life choices based on what would please Him. I'm a lot like Mom now. I make careful choices based on what I believe is "just perfect" for the person or situation involved. And I try to remember that my choices reveal my heart.

I have a picture hanging in my living room depicting Mary, Joseph, and baby Jesus. I leave it up year-round. Though I chose it as a "Christmas decoration," that isn't what it has become to me. It's a constant reminder that Jesus came as Immanuel, God with us. He chose to send His Son. Jesus was God wrapped in swaddling clothes for Mary and Joseph. He is God with me today. He is still Immanuel.

Have you ever wondered why God chose to step down into the middle of the mess man had made of creation to be with us? I wonder about that sometimes, especially in my less-than-masterpiece moments. The only answer is that He did it entirely for us. He sent what was perfect to redeem the imperfect. His example is echoed by Hallmark's advertising slogan. He did it because He cares enough to send the very best. So, the answer to my question, "why?" Because: *God so loved the world that He gave His one and only Son...* (Jo 3:16 NIV). Hallmark offers nothing comparable! He gave the very best because He cares that much.

It's easy for us to miss the message that, for God, this life is all about relationship. He didn't create inanimate artistic masterpieces to place in museums. He created man in His image to look, live, and love like He does. Out of all creation, we–you and I—are the ones He handcrafted specifically to share relationship with Him. And literally everything He has done since has been to restore us to that original design.

God's plan has always been that we become more and more like our Father, like Him. He knows that *...bad company corrupts good character* (1Co 15:33 NKJV), but godly character is even more contagious. There had to be a plan to protect us from the bad company of the world. The plan was Jesus. He came to be **with us**. The more time we spend with Him, the more we will think, act, and live like Him.

In your quest to take ownership of your identity in Christ, realize you are not self-made. Even a "good" Christian's value is not in her own nature or abilities. It is *Christ in you, the hope of glory* (Co 1:27 NIV). That takes the pressure off! Christ in you is the definition of being a masterpiece; it is God-with-us that transforms us from the world's mess to what God so loved He gave to save.

My memories from today's moments with the Master...

_____

_____

_____

Conversation with the Master…

I am amazed, Lord, that you loved me so much that you cared enough to send the very best: Your Your Son, Emmanuel… God With Us. And because of that, my mess is transformed to masterpiece. Thank you for being the very best… God with me… Emmanuel!

DAY 11
AN ATTITUDE ADJUSTMENT

> *Do not urge me to leave you or to turn back from following you; for where you go, I will go, and where you lodge, I will lodge. Your people will be my people, and your God, my God.* (Ru 1:16 TPT).

There are people who make my life better just by being a part of it. When I hear their name, I smile. When my caller ID says they are calling, I answer quickly. When I spend time with them, I feel better and laugh more. When I need help, support, or encouragement, they're the ones I turn to.

Some people might call these people "besties," or best friends, but that implies negative comparison with others. It isn't how they compare to "non-besties," but what they add to my life that matters. True friends are the indefinable ingredient that makes the whole dish of life better. It isn't what they do or the things they add, but the attitude they bring that transforms the atmosphere around them. We all want to know that kind of person. We should all **be** that person in the lives of the people around us.

I believe that is the kind of person the Bible story of Ruth reveals. I've always been intrigued by her. She has a book in the Old Testament named after her, yet she was not a Jew. She was given the option to remain in her hometown with her family, but she chose to leave; she decided to go with Naomi, yet Naomi did nothing to encourage her. She left everything familiar for a place she'd never been, with a woman who chose to name herself Mara, which means Bitter. From all appearances, this was not the recipe for a joyful journey. Why would a young widow choose Bethlehem over Moab, Mara over her mother, and moving to a strange place over what was safe and familiar?

Listen carefully to Ruth's words in our verse today. You can hear her heart and understand her why's. She was committed to the relationship. She was choosing the challenge. She was moving ahead without a map.

I have made quite a few moves in my life…about 20 if I remember correctly. Some of those were very difficult, some were exciting; but all were defined more by my attitude than by the circumstances. When my family made our first major move I was 12, I was totally ignorant about the process. I remember thinking moving would be a great escape. New friends wouldn't know my history—all the dumb or clumsy things I had done in the past and would prefer others forget. Clearly, my self-image was poor.

There is a saying: "Wherever you go, there you are." Wherever I moved, regardless how many friends I met, I took with me, packed not in a box but in my heart, **me**. My attitude largely determined my experience. Like me, there may be things about yourself you would like to change; it may appear moving, even running, might be a relief. But the same attitude in a new location will have the same, or very similar, results.

Life is an overarching transition to destiny comprised of changes, transformations, and adaptation. Each one moves us from one place to another, one season to another, one level to another, even one relationship to another. But it is our attitude that shapes the transition, not the opposite. Are you settling for a temporary destination, or are you reaching for your eternal destiny? Your answer will be determined by your attitude.

Ruth is a powerful example of choosing not to be defined by the stops along the journey, but by the destiny to which it led. She could have chosen to have a bad attitude, like her mother-in-law who chose to be Bitter Mara over Sweet Naomi. If only Naomi could have read Romans 12:2 (NASB): *And do not be conformed to this world, but be transformed by the renewing of your mind, so that you may prove what the will of God is, that which is good and acceptable and perfect.*

Her personal instruction could have read: "Be not conformed to the attitude of bitter but transformed into the attitude of better." (The Carol Revised Version)

Do you realize you are God's creative masterpiece wherever you are? Geography doesn't determine masterpiece status. You can't transition enough, make enough moves, hide behind enough makeovers to alter the unchangeable fact that God still sees you as He created you to be…His masterpiece. What others say or think, or how you see yourself, doesn't change your image in His eyes. He celebrates what He knows. And he knows the destiny for which you were created.

When God created man He said, "It is very good!"—His highest rating for any of His creation! He celebrated the person He had made. He still does. People around you may celebrate you or tolerate you. Your attitude will determine which you allow to define you.

> *I praise you because I am fearfully and wonderfully made; your works are wonderful, I know that full well* (Ps 139:14 <u>NIV</u>).

Know you're a masterpiece and celebrate it…with the Master.

My memories from today's moments with the Master…

_____

_____

_____

Conversation with the Master…

> *Like the psalmist David, I praise You for creating me to be a masterpiece, "fearfully and wonderfully made." I choose today to celebrate my masterpiece status and to develop an attitude like Ruth's of better, not bitter.*

DAY 12
DISTRACTED BY THE MASTER

But Martha was distracted with all her preparations (Lu 10:40 NASB).

I am easily distracted…especially by clutter or disorganization. I can leave the living room to find my glasses…notice dishes are stacking up in the kitchen sink…unload the dishwasher so I can load the dishes…realize we are out of paper towels by the sink, so go to the garage to grab some…only to see the freezer in the garage and decide to bring in some meat to thaw for dinner…forget the towels…go back in with the meat only to realize there is still a pile of dirty dishes and still no paper towels….and I still don't have my glasses. I think you get the idea. Distracted. Distraction derails fixed focus.

In just five verses, Luke 10:38-42 reveals the dangers of distraction and the blessing of fixed focus. Martha welcomed Jesus into her home, and then apparently rushed off to fulfill her responsibilities. But her sister, Mary, couldn't get enough of time with Jesus. Can you picture the scene? Mary is sitting as close as she can get to Jesus. Martha is chasing around doing all the things. I can imagine her popping through the doorway occasionally to glare and clear her throat loudly, assuming she can get Mary's attention and some help. Maybe she even stomped away loudly, hoping that would communicate her righteous indignation. But no.

In absolute frustration, Martha vented on Jesus. "Don't you care?!!!!" (I'm sure there were a bunch of exclamation points after her question.) Seriously? Martha questioned if Jesus cared? Yes! Yes she did. She had been serving all alone, probably working up a sweat along with a head of steam. She wanted someone to do something about her situation.

I don't know how you imagine Jesus, but I always think of Him as having kind yet piercing eyes, eyes that looked right past masks and pretense and into hearts. After Martha's tirade, he spoke her name…twice. He wanted her to know He knew her, saw her, and wanted something better for her. Martha's emotional diet of worry, bother, and anxiety was the exact opposite of what He offered. He wanted her to have the best: time with Him.

I wonder if I would behave more like Mary or Martha if Jesus were to come my house for dinner and a visit. I would like to think I would be a Mary who set aside everything else and was distracted only by Him. But realistically, I know I can be easily sidetracked like Martha by serving rather than focusing on the Savior—sadly, giving Him second place in my thoughts and attention. In my rush to extend hospitality, my priorities could become skewed to **doing** rather than **being**. I might forget the Master is more important than any masterpiece I might create in the kitchen, how beautifully the table is set, or how clean the house is. But worse, I could forget He wants my presence more than my presents, my heart more than my help.

When our daughter was in her late teens she attended a boot camp-style discipleship training program. Every morning the campers were required to start their day very early spending hours in prayer and Bible reading. Several days into this program her dad called to check on her. He was thrilled when she told him, "Dad, today we were playing volleyball after our prayer and study time. I couldn't play. I just had to leave the game because I was distracted by God."

How often in the busyness of life do you find yourself distracted by God? Do memories of time with Him cause you to push aside the urgent demands of your day to do what is most important—to spend time with Him? Your relationship with Him deepens as He becomes, not a habit, but the necessity of your life. When we take time to listen, we know His heart. When hearing becomes obedience, we please Him. Knowing Him becomes not our to-do list, but rather who we are.

> *Has the Lord as great delight in burnt offerings and sacrifices, as in obeying the voice of the Lord? Behold, to obey is better than sacrifice, and to listen than the fat of rams* (1Sa 15:22 ESV).

God is delighted when we hear and obey His voice. However, He gives us freedom to make that choice…Mary or Martha? Delight or disappoint?

It's up to you. Choose today to be a delightful masterpiece distracted by the Master.

My memories from today's moments with the Master…

_____

_____

_____

Conversation with the Master…

> *I want You, Lord, to be my focus. Draw me close to Your side where I can **be** what You created me to be: Your masterpiece. I want to be present in the moment with You, not distracted by what I am doing, but delighting You by being still in Your presence.*

DAY 13
BORN TO SERVE THE LORD

For we are his workmanship, created in Christ Jesus for good works, which God prepared beforehand so that we would walk in them (Eph 2:10 NKJV).

I began taking piano lessons when I was about ten years old. Though I didn't pursue it for long, I learned enough to play by written notes from simple songbooks. And I enjoyed it. Probably because she loved me no matter what, my mom enjoyed my playing, too. Often, when I would go to the piano, she would call in to me, "Play your song for me." I knew what she wanted. It was a Bill Gaither song called "Born to Serve the Lord." Looking back, I realize she loved hearing me play that song because that is how she saw me. As the one who gave me physical life, she recognized my true Source of life, life in the Spirit.

The chorus of the song said, "For I was made in His likeness, created in His image. For I was born to serve the Lord; and I can't deny Him, I'll always walk beside Him, for I was born to serve the Lord." Mom knew why I had been born, and she claimed this as my testimony. Every time I played and sang this song, I was testifying that I was His masterpiece born to serve my Master.

Years have passed. Mom is in heaven now. But engraved on my heart is the truth that she knew: I was born to serve the Lord. I am His masterpiece. The more I claim it, the more I walk in it.

The people around you may try to convince you that you are not a masterpiece. Often, for their own selfish reasons, they will point out your weaknesses, criticize your abilities, and underestimate your strength. Why? Because Satan's strategy is to cause you to remember your past failures, focus on your inadequacies, and fear your future.

You don't live in yesterday; don't be defined by it, nor by today's circumstances. And don't make choices for your future out of fear or feelings of inadequacy. *Choose for yourselves today whom you will serve: whether the gods which your fathers served which were beyond the river, or the gods of the Amorites in whose land you are living; but as for me and my house, we will serve the Lord* (Jos 24:15 NASB).

Joshua was talking to a group of people who had to choose to win over continuing to wander. They could long for what they left behind in their past (Egypt), fear the giants they faced today, or claim the future God promised. We still have those choices to make. We can be and do what we were born for….or not.

Sometimes, even when we believe we are doing what we are supposed to be doing, it doesn't feel that way at all. We can get into situations that are not only uncomfortable, but painful. When things are not going as we had envisioned them, we begin questioning the choices that got us here.

That reminds me of when I was in seventh grade and had just moved…a move from a small town to a city, from childhood friends to knowing no one, from familiar to very strange. I had spent six years in one school. Over the next six years I attended eight different schools. New places. New friends. New experiences. What at first seemed like a great way to get away from the embarrassments of past goof-ups, became a test I hadn't prepared to take. I was **not** convinced I was born to serve like **that**.

But pain often has purpose. My Provider had both a plan and a purpose. I had to learn that it wasn't up to me to figure it all out. I had to accept that my comfort wasn't the point. Eventually, it was a proverb that became my path through the pain and into His plan: *Trust in the Lord with all your heart and lean not on your own understanding; in all your ways acknowledge Him, and He shall direct your paths* (Pr 3:5,6 NKJV).

To discover what I had truly been born for required that I trust God enough to stay on the path, out of my own head, and committed to the journey I was taking.

The Master gives direction, not a full script for the story of our lives. We must learn to simply trust Him, not necessarily understand what He's up to. The more we say, "He's in charge and I trust Him," the more we open ourselves to His leading.

What were you born to do? Does that question scare you just a little? Great big life questions like that can overwhelm us if we insist on putting ourselves in the equation for working out solutions for our problems. But remove your control from the equation and allow God to use you for service in the way He "prepared beforehand" for you to walk. That will take you from being the weakest link in the chain to being the masterpiece you were created to be. Just focus on what you were born for! Serving Him. He takes care of the details.

My memories from today's moments with the Master…

_____

_____

_____

Conversation with the Master…

> *Lord, some days I forget that my purpose in living is to serve You. Teach me to trust You, to lean on Your wisdom, and to acknowledge You in all my ways. Lead me on Your path. I choose to live in Your plan as Your masterpiece. That is what I was born to do.*

DAY 14
NEVER AND NOW

"We who have run for our very lives to God have every reason to grab the promised hope with both hands and never let go. It's an unbreakable spiritual lifeline, reaching past all appearances right to the very presence of God where Jesus, running on ahead of us has taken up His permanent post as high priest for us... (He 6:18b-20 MSG).

Some days I get lost in neverland. It's not an amusement park, not even close. In fact, it's not even a real place. It's that place in my mind where all I can hear is the voice telling me, "You'll **never** be able to reach that goal." "You **never** succeed; why even try?" "You'll **never** be as beautiful as she is." And on, and on, and on. Whenever I hear "never" I know I'm not hearing from God. At any right-now moment I can be defeated by "never." You see, "never" never comes, but "right now" is a new gift created just for me by the Creator of always. *The steadfast love of the Lord never ceases; his mercies never come to an end; they are new every morning* (La 3:22, 23 ESV). The world's "nevers" stop me; they attempt to control me. But God's "always" propels me forward with promise.

As we move forward in God's plan for us, life can become a road on which we are constantly confronted with a choice at the intersection of "Never Street" and "Now Road." The flesh, our human nature, finds it so much easier and less risky, to believe in "never" than to accept by faith God's "now."

But for every "never" moment the world offers, God throws out "now" lifelines. He reminds you and me that He is with us always, despite what "now" looks like from our perspective. *Be strong and courageous. Do not be afraid or terrified…for the Lord your God goes with you; he will never leave you nor forsake you* (Dt 31:6 NIV).

I have experienced some scary "now" moments. I can picture clearly in my mind where I was standing in my kitchen one sunny afternoon when I heard over the phone a nurse reporting test results that said, "Cancer." I was flooded with the possibility of "never."

I've learned since that day that cancer is a name, a name for a terrible disease, but one over which I can speak the name of Jesus. His name wins. *Therefore God has highly exalted him and bestowed on him the name that is above every name, so that at the name of Jesus every knee should bow, in heaven and on earth and under the earth, and every tongue confess that Jesus Christ is Lord, to the glory of God the Father* (Ph 2:9-11 ESV).

That day I began developing faith in the power of God to turn "never" into "now." My mind scrolled down through a seemingly endless list of possible "nevers": I'll never see my daughters grow up…never see them get married…I'll never fulfill all my dreams, never grow old. However, over the course of a few months, I saw those fears disappear as by the power of the name of Jesus I was healed. Nearly 30 years later, I am still living in God's now. I am healed, whole, and chasing God-given dreams. He confirmed His promise: *And my God will liberally supply (fill until full) your every need according to his riches in glory in Christ Jesus"* (Ph 4:19 AMP).

Are you feeling overwhelmed by all the "nevers" that keep popping up in your life? Maybe you feel you will never catch up on the bills that need to be paid. Or perhaps you believe you can never forgive the person who has hurt you deeply. Whether it's finances, relationships, dreams, or diets with which you are struggling, God still promises only good "nevers" for you: I'm not leaving you. I promise I will never abandon you nor leave you behind. I will never turn My back on you nor give up on you. I am 100% with you 100% of the time. Circumstances don't change Me or My plan for you, my masterpiece.

Turned over to Him, my temporary "nevers" are transformed into an eternal "now."

The best never ever is that God never stops loving us. Love is who He is and what He does. That unfailing love is a lifeline of truth in this world's sea of lies. Remember, Satan is a liar, has always lied, doesn't do anything but lie. If he's saying it, it can't be true. If you hear him say "never," start holding the lifeline of the Master's love now.

In the middle of your mess, you can grab hold of that promise and be pulled to safety—NOW. You may feel as if you're going under; you may not be able to see the safe place to which you are being drawn. But God's lifeline is hope, no matter what the circumstances appear to be. He is always pulling the ones He loves to safety. He is always shaping and caring for His masterpiece. He lifts us up above all the tangled mess of Satan's lies with our lifeline anchored to hope…and hope in God always wins.

My memories from today's moments with the Master…

_____

_____

_____

Conversation with the Master…

> *You, Lord, are my lifeline of hope. There are voices all around me that say I will **never** be enough, **never** have enough, **never** do enough. But Your Word tells me that You will make me enough; You will supply my every need not based on what I have, but from Your riches in glory. Thank You for being my more-than-enough and my lifeline of hope.*

DAY 15
WHEN THE MASTER SPEAKS

Be still and realize that I am God (Ps 46:10 TPT).

I am a planner and a list maker. I love having a to-do list and checking things off. But some days my list is too long. Some days my mind needs rest rather than another check mark on my list. Sometimes life can become too much! Days can be packed full of busy. Nights no longer bring sweet rest but are merely one more venue in which to rehash and fight again the day's battles.

On those days, I need to stop and listen…listen to the one voice that restores my mess back into masterpiece order. If I want peace, I must return to the Peacemaker, the Master of quiet, the One Who can soothe my frantic mind.

> *You will keep in perfect and constant peace the one whose mind is steadfast [that is, committed and focused on You—in both inclination and character], because he trusts and takes refuge in you [with hope and confident expectation]* (Is 26:3 AMP).

Do you ever find yourself so ruled by busy, so tied up in emotional knots, so full of anxiety, that your spiritual ears become stopped up with all that and you can't hear God's voice…in fact nearly forget what it sounds like? I can't lie. I have found myself there. And I don't like it!

The dangerous truth is, in that moment, we forget who God is. Our only hope lies in being still and realizing He is still God. And He has the only answer for our rapid freefall into anxiety, fear, and despair.

He whispers quietly into our spirit: "I will keep you in perfect peace, just focus on me. Trust me. Put your hope and confidence in Me. Be still and listen. The psalmist heard and understood: *Be still and know that I am God* (Ps 46:10 NLT).

How long has it been since you pulled away from everything that is distracting you from your Master and were still…quiet in His presence…open to His message…made complete in His love? In the middle of the chaos of your life, do you run to Him as your refuge? Today may be the day for you to rediscover your connection to peace.

There was an ad campaign several years ago by a financial planning advisor that said, "When E.F. Hutton talks, people listen." It showed people literally stopping everything they were doing and physically leaning in to hear. When you believe someone has answers you need, you stop, listen, and follow instructions. God is the planner for all eternity. His design has never failed. Everything He touches becomes a masterpiece. And yet, are we leaning in to hear what He says? If not, why not?

Remember the parable Jesus told in Matthew 13 about the seed being sown in different types of soil? Which one describes the soil of your life?

> *The one sown among thorns represents one who receives the message, but all of life's busy distractions, his divided heart, and his ambition for wealth result in suffocating the kingdom message and it becomes fruitless. But what was sown on good, rich soil represents the one who hears and fully embraces the message of the kingdom. Their lives bear good fruit"* (Mt 13:22, 23 TPT).

God's kingdom message is the same seed in both cases, but the reception for the seed makes all the difference. We become hearing impaired when we allow "life's busy distractions," like confusion and the drive for success to drown out God's voice. If you want a fruitful life, the seed is available. But your response must be to turn away from distractions, to open your heart and mind, and to focus on the plan.

Jesus is our pattern; when He was here on earth, He followed that plan. *But Jesus himself would often slip away to the wilderness and pray* (Lu 5:16 NASB).

When God talks, we may miss His voice unless we have learned to ditch all the demanding details and distracting diversions that can easily develop in our lives.

> *Come close to God, and God will come close to you. Wash your hands, you sinners; purify your hearts, for your loyalty is divided between God and the world* (Ja 4:8 NLT).

When the Master speaks, His true masterpieces listen!
My memories from today's moments with the Master...

_____

_____

_____

Conversation with the Master...

> *Teach me, Master, to lean in and listen to Your voice. There is so much noise and chaos surrounding me. I want to "be still and know" You. Even in this moment, help me to step out of the mess and listen to the Master. When I'm tempted to pull away, draw me close to You where I can listen for your heartbeat and hear your voice.*

DAY 16

MASTERPIECE IN MOTION

I press on toward the goal to win the prize (Ph 3:14 <u>NIV</u>*).*

Do you ever have "terrible, horrible, no good, very bad days" like Alexander in Judith Viorst's children's book? Sometimes I do, not often, but occasionally. In fact, occasionally I also remind myself of Eeyore in *Winnie the Pooh*. The poor guy has such a hard time finding his happy! Once, offered a change, he replied, "Thanks, but I'd rather stay an Eeyore." Sadly, sometimes when we are having a bad day we prefer to stay in the mess we know rather than do the hard work of growing into the masterpiece we are destined to become.

God doesn't see any of us as a hopeless Eeyore. If we see ourselves that way, it is because our focus is on our circumstances and not on God's point of view. I have realized that often when I feel I have fallen too far short of what God expects of me it is because I am focused on where I am now, while He sees me as He created me to be.

Life is a journey. Sometimes it resembles a family road trip. It begins with high expectations for all the exciting things ahead. But the process of getting to the exciting part is the problem. A few miles into the trip a little voice from the back seat whines, "Are we there yet?" The answer is, "No, not yet." The operative word in that reply is "yet."

If you're a masterpiece-in-the-making, if you're having a no good very bad day, if you're just not "there yet," there's still hope. Your destiny is still ahead. The apostle Paul understood this. He explained, *Not that I have already obtained all this, or have already arrived at my goal, but I press on to take hold of that for which Christ Jesus took hold of me"* (Ph 3:12 NIV).

Pressing on is generally required to reach a promise. Along the way there may very well be some no good, even very bad, days. I'm reminded of Peter. He had "one of those days." Read Matthew 14:22-33. This a very familiar story. Though we tend to remember only the miracle, in real time Peter was a bit of a mess.

I'm guessing he and the other disciples were pretty worn out after serving 5000+ people the bread and fish and then cleaning up the leftovers. Jesus surely recognized their weariness, because in verse 22 (NIV) it says, *Immediately Jesus made the disciples get into the boat and go on ahead of him to the other side.* I can imagine Him giving the same sigh of relief a parent in the front seat lets out when the kids finally fall asleep, and the questions are quieted. A little time on the mountain by himself to pray was undoubtedly refreshing.

The disciples, though, didn't even have time to rest from the outdoor kitchen duty when a storm came up. I can imagine Peter: "Oh great! First a feeding frenzy and now this! Did you see that wave! Will this day ever end???" Then, he saw Jesus! On the water! Hope was walking on the waves. Peter got out, started well, and then sank. At that moment, he had the option to remain Peter the mess, or take Jesus' hand and be changed to Peter the Masterpiece…even if it was a masterpiece in progress, dripping wet, and maybe shaking. Jesus saw him as safe. And he was.

We are most familiar with completed masterpieces, those at the end of their process. They are on public display only after all the rough spots are smoothed away, the colors blended, the script edited and polished, the production rehearsed and perfected. The process is, in the end, invisible. No one is aware of how many attempts the master powered through to achieve the plan from which the final product emerged.

Michelangelo painted for four years on the ceiling of the Sistine Chapel. Leonardo DaVinci painted for 16 years to completing the Mona Lisa. The Hope Diamond took from the mid-1600's in India until 1968 to reach the Smithsonian Institution, where it is on display and considered a prime exhibit today. Through all those years it was sold and resold, cut and recut, mounted on crowns and suspended on gold chains. It was owned by French royalty and New York socialites. It was a masterpiece in motion.

All masterpieces move through stages. They are developed, perfected, and treasured. The journey from beginning to end may be long, tedious, and difficult. In the end, for the masterpiece, the story of its journey may be as valuable and precious as the final destination.

Your story, your testimony, matters. It is your journey from your beginning in the mind of God, through all the twists and turns of life, past failure, and into your future. It is the story of the masterpiece that is you and bears the name of the Master.

My memories from today's moments with the Master…

_____

_____

_____

Conversation with the Master…

Lord, I'm asking You to help me remember that in the middle of no good, very bad days You are still with me. Even if I'm going down in the waves, You are still reaching out to me. I make my decision in advance: I will press on to take hold of Your hand even when it feels as if I am sinking; I will be the masterpiece You have designed me to be.

DAY 17
JESUS THE MASTER INFLUENCER

For I did not speak on my own, but the Father who sent me commanded me to say all that I have spoken. I know that his command leads to eternal life. So whatever I say is just what the Father has told me to say (Jo 12:49-50 NIV).

The internet changed my world while I wasn't looking. I barely noticed when roadmaps were replaced by the GPS on my phone. I was totally unaware when encyclopedias and other reference books were replaced by Google. (Who knew so many of life's questions could be answered by "googling it?" In fact, who knew "googling" would be a word?) And recently I discovered another introduction to my world: influencers. They were busy speaking into my life long before I realized they existed! Have you noticed the influencers in your life?

According to my research, the concept of influencers began in the late 1980s with the introduction of the internet. There was a time, believe it or not, when the World Wide Web wasn't a thing! It was created in 1989 by a British guy named Tim Berners-Lee working in Switzerland. Within ten years that creation exploded in influence. Digital bloggers became internet celebrities and people began following their every word, being influenced in whatever direction they were led. It didn't take long for someone to realize if they paid the messenger/influencer, they controlled the message, and their own message spread as their profits increased.

As I've studied this trend, I've concluded that this is not truly a new thing. Jesus was the original influencer. He came with a message…one

His Father sent Him to share. He said what His Father told Him to say. But rather than using His influence to become rich, He was using it to share His riches. He came to meet needs, not create them. *And my God will supply all your needs according to his riches in glory in Christ Jesus* (Ph 4:19 NASB).

His influence wasn't bought and paid for by a profit-motivated sponsor. Instead, He came to pay for everything we would ever need…out of His own supply, His riches in glory.

Aren't you thankful you were introduced to a God whose relationship with you is about making you His personal masterpiece rather than using you to enrich Himself? He came to give life, not suck the life out of us. I am refreshed by that! In a world where I often feel used, where it seems the more I give the more is demanded, where people are more interested in the financial bottom line than in extending a lifeline of relationship, Jesus is all about giving life, hope, and freedom.

> *The thief comes only to steal and kill and destroy; I have come that they may have life, and have it to the full* (Jo 10:10 NIV).

Jesus influences not for a sponsor, but as a Savior. He isn't out to get you, but to give you life. While influencers create an insatiable hunger for more, better, different, Jesus satisfies at a level so deep we will never need more than He is.

The influencers of the world work subtly. They don't always reveal their purpose. Remember, the thief doesn't give notice that he is coming after your stuff. He doesn't tell you that the consequence of letting him in may be losing your life. He certainly doesn't let you know in advance that you are disposable after use. The world and its sponsor, Satan, use their influence in your life to steal your joy, kill your hope, and destroy your eternity.

As the Creator's masterpiece, I am an influencer for Him. I follow Jesus' example. I discover in His Word a complete Masterpiece Training program. I carry His name. I receive His riches. I communicate His message of love and share His gift of salvation. I can do all that only because I am under the influence—the influence of the Master Influencer.

There is life, amazing, limitless life, in that choice.

People constantly receive messages from internet influencers, from movie characters, from popular entertainers, from TV stars. Those influencers offer all sorts of stuff. And it is easy to be distracted by the things they offer. But look behind the script, past their appearances, into their eyes where their hearts are revealed. For many of them, Satan's influence has left them empty, lost, and always seeking something more, something—anything—that will satisfy and last.

I find my answer for all that in an old, old song which we sang in church when I was growing up. It was written by Helen Howarth Lemmel, and inspired by (influenced by!) missionary Isabella Lilias Trotter. It said, "Turn your eyes upon Jesus. Look full in His wonderful face; and the things of earth will grow strangely dim in the light of His glory and grace."

Today, simply shift your focus to Jesus. In following Him, you find all you need…all you will ever need.

My memories from today's moments with the Master…

_____

_____

_____

Conversation with the Master…

Father, teach me to be an influencer for Your kingdom—for Your glory, not mine. I will live to follow Jesus' example as an influencer in my world for You. Help me to become more like Him…doing what You do and saying what You say. I will live under Your influence.

DAY 18
MESSES CAN BE MASTERPIECES

On the Lord's Day I [John] was in the Spirit, and I heard behind me a loud voice like a trumpet, which said: "Write… (Re 1:10, 11 <u>NIV</u>).

I'm sure not everyone who reads the Revelation is smacked in the face by this passage like I am. God uses it to remind me what I was created for and what my assignment is from Him. I am, like John the writer of the Revelation, called to write. I know that. Often, however, I fail to feel it. He reminds me—much more often than is comfortable—that feelings are not how this works. His plan is for willing obedience, not necessarily my comfort level.

Maybe you are thinking, "But I've never heard a loud voice like a trumpet telling me what to do." Well, most of us never do. More often, God's calling is more like a gentle nudge or a soft word of assurance, an unexpected success at something we were drawn to do but didn't attempt previously for fear of failure. Moving from making messes to creating masterpieces is a process. We learn to walk in our calling like a baby learns to walk…one fall after another until finally the steps replace falls and the child becomes a walker—maybe a toddler, but still a walker.

You and I can be encouraged by John the Writer. He didn't start out with a heavenly writing assignment. Years before, I'm sure that the fisherman Jesus found fishing and called to be a disciple was not planning a career as a writer. He knew how to take orders, but receive an assignment to write for God? Not him! He was a worker. He and his brother James were nicknamed Sons of Thunder for a reason. They handled heavy nets and sails, not nouns, verbs and punctuation. They were probably known more for their brawn than for their brains.

So, imagine the miracle of being the one through whom God chose to reveal himself and His plan to man! I have wondered why John was chosen for this writing project. Why not Paul? He seems an obvious choice to me. We will never know for sure. In the end, however, it was Jesus' buddy, the blustering fisherman turned loyal, faithful, and loving disciple who was commissioned.

At some point he was ready to write.

You may feel as if you're neither ready nor qualified to do anything for the Kingdom. As you have read up to this point today you may have thought, "I'm not called to do anything like that!" And you're right. Because God doesn't need a whole kingdom of Johns or Carols. He needs you! You are called. You are gifted. God specifically created you to fulfill a specific role among His disciples. He knows what boat you're working on, and He has already determined to repurpose you for new service for Him as you follow and obey. He made John a fisher of men. He has no problem making you what you are destined to become.

John the writer of the Revelation wrote from the Island of Patmos where he was exiled for preaching the Gospel. It was not exactly a place oozing with inspiration, furnished with ergonomic writing equipment, and decorated with encouraging scripture plaques. But who He knew was more important than where he was. Even in exile, he hadn't forgotten to focus on the Master. On the Lord's Day he was probably worshiping, because we know he says he was "in the spirit." What a strong reminder that the most powerful and rewarding times of our life will be experienced when we put ourselves in a position to not only hear the voice of God, but truly listen, and put ourselves in His hands.

It is, after all, the Master's touch that changes art materials or random words into masterpieces of design, color, function, and beauty. Lumps of clay become beautiful pottery in the hands of the potter. Blank canvases transform into amazing expressions of a painter's vision. Carefully crafted scripts come to life on a stage as the playwright's words capture the imagination of an audience.

Maybe John had learned this lesson of transformation from the psalms he had studied as a boy. Many of those psalms told the story of the life of David. He was revealed as a poet, a musician, a writer of music and of lyrics. He was even called a man after God's own heart. But he had his own Island of Patmos moments. At one time He was a shepherd boy out in the fields doing the lonely job of herding sheep. Later, he was a fugitive hiding in a cave and running from a crazed king. He was an anointed king leading a band of losers and misfits. But no matter where he was, how messy life looked, He trusted the Master Plan: *When you created me in the secret place…carefully, skillfully you shaped me from nothing to something* (Ps 139:15 TPT).

Today, trust the Master with your nothing mess and He will carefully and skillfully change that mess into something masterful!

My memories from today's moments with the Master…

_____

_____

_____

Conversation with the Master…

Lord, Your Word teaches me You created me in the secret place and skillfully shaped me. Still, You know how messy my life is. On my own, transformation is impossible. But Your Word teaches me that I can trust You to shape my mess into Your masterpiece. That is what I am trusting you to do—today and all my tomorrows.

DAY 19
WITH THIS RING

[God] knows we are his since he has also stamped his seal of love over our hearts and has given us the Holy Spirit like an engagement ring is given to a bride—a down payment of the blessings to come (2Co 1:22 TPT)!

God is the Great Romantic. By definition that means He is "characterized by the expression of love." (from Oxford Languages) I like that! A lot! As a little girl I memorized 1 John 4:8: *God is love.* It was short, sweet and to the point. That verse worked for me then, and it still does. It puts in three words a truth that, if accepted wholeheartedly, makes sense out of life. Everything in all creation for all time has resulted from that one truth. It confirms that what matters most to God is His relationship with us. The Master loves His masterpieces.

Maybe the fact that I am loved by a man who is very romantic factors into my response. He reminds me frequently that I am not my own because God and his dad (who performed our wedding ceremony) gave me to him. The beautiful ring I wear on my left hand is a message from him to me of his love and to others that I am his. When he slipped that ring on my finger it was a sort of "down payment of the blessings to come." It is a sign of the covenant bond that unites us.

Throughout the Bible, God's message to man is that He loves us and that He is committed to us by covenant—a covenant He will never break. As a sign, to seal the deal with us, he has given us the Holy Spirit; His

Spirit isn't just a ring on our finger, but a sign of who God is in and for us…much like the Master's signature on a masterpiece.

Maybe life hasn't always been a series of romantic moments and tender love for you. In fact, maybe reading this makes you uncomfortable. It may remind you of all the broken promises you have been given. Memories of lies, betrayal, pain, and manipulation may make trust impossible. For you, romantic love stories are cruel reminders of love you lost, or maybe never had.

You may consider yourself a ruined or discarded masterpiece tossed in life's trash dumpster. But you need to realize God will never see you that way. Because He loves you, He understands. Even now, after all you have gone through, His commitment to you remains. He is still love wrapping its arms around you. He reminds you "I am" when you can only think of what you are not. *The Lord is near to the brokenhearted and saves those who are crushed in spirit* (Ps 34:18 NASB).

There are countless stories of artists who spend untold hours slaving over a masterpiece, and suddenly devastation strikes…the canvas tears, the clay cracks, the script is burned, the diamond is lost…and it appears nothing is left but to start over. Our Master never gives up. His deep commitment to the forming of the masterpiece causes Him to reimagine, restore, recreate. He reaffirms His promise: to love despite circumstances, to make something out of nothing, to love without limit. And in those times, He speaks gently to His handiwork, *See, I am doing a new thing! Now it springs up; do you not perceive it? I am making a way…* (Is 43:19 NIV).

The past isn't a problem for the Master. If necessary, He will start over. He will mend the torn canvas; the broken places in life will be covered by new blessing. He will rework the clay; the new creation will reflect His love and skill, not the damage of the past. He preserves the master copy of the script of your life; it will reveal beauty you only dreamed of in the past. Because He knows all things, though it seemed the diamond was lost and would never sparkle again, He will not only find it, but repolish, remount, and reveal the stone of great value He saw all along.

We live in a throwaway world. When something doesn't work the way we want, we trash it. When a couple becomes disappointed with their mate, they divorce. When a device becomes outdated, it is stuck in the back of a closet, replaced by the next latest and greatest, which will be in the closet, too, before long.

God never throws away the ones He created, the masterpieces on which He has signed His name. His Spirit in us means that rather than rejecting us and moving on, He restores us to original specifications. And no matter how many times we feel as if we don't deserve the love, and should probably return the ring, He loves. In fact, He **is** love, remember? *The steadfast love of the Lord never ceases; his mercies never come to an end; they are new every morning"* (La 3:22-23 ESV).

Because we wear His ring, we are stamped by His love. We are "in a relationship"—permanently. And the Holy Spirit in us is a promise, a down payment, on blessings to come. Get ready for the blessing!

My memories from today's moments with the Master…

_____

_____

_____

Conversation with the Master…

> *God, I am so thankful that You don't throw away broken people. I find hope in knowing You are doing "a new thing" when I feel as if I am beyond repair. I believe that Your love never ceases and that every morning is another opportunity to receive Your love and mercy. Here I am, ready to receive Your blessing of love.*

DAY 20

I'VE BEEN FRAMED!

> *By faith we understand that the worlds were framed by the word of God, so that the things which are seen were not made of things which are visible."* (He 11:3 NKJV).

You have been framed…and that's not a bad thing! In so many ways, life depends on frames. Look at the definitions of the word frame. The first is: "a rigid structure that surrounds or encloses something." ("frame; *www.dictionary.com*) In Hebrews 11:3 God is the invisible frame that surrounds and holds everything together; He is the unseen force framing all of creation.

I love how Paul explains this: *And He Himself existed and is before all things, and in Him all things hold together [His is the controlling, cohesive force of the universe]* (Col 1:17 AMP).

I'm pretty sure that if the universe would literally fly apart without the frame of His presence, we need His surrounding boundary as well. The frame is our Friend! He holds us together.

The second definition given of frame is: "A case or border enclosing a mirror or picture." As I write this, I am surrounded by framed pictures. Without the frames the pictures wouldn't have the structure or support to stand on their own. They wouldn't have a place specially designed and chosen for them. They wouldn't be protected. The right frame makes the picture look better! God, holding us within the borders and boundaries of His love for us, reveals us to the world as His masterpiece.

The third definition of frame is, "the rigid supporting structure of an object such as a vehicle, building, or piece of furniture." This framework is internal, generally unseen, but always necessary. Whether it's a car, a castle, or a couch, everything made needs a framework that defines its identity. For us, that framework is the Word. Just as words gave life to creation, the Word is the lifegiving framework upon which our life is built. Without it there is no structure and no support. Without that framework, life is a lot like building a house out of Jell-O. An unmoving, unchanging framework of the Word holds us in right relationship with God. *Your word I have hidden in my heart, that I might not sin against You* (Ps 119:11 NKJV).

Basically, sin is separation from God. When we are separated from our structure, we collapse. Being framed is not optional. Without the structure of the Word upon which believers build their lives, there is no strength or preventative planning to enable them to stand against temptation.

I really like the picture of a frame expressed by the last definition given: "a boxlike structure in which seeds or young plants are grown." God is the safe box in which we can grow and develop. He surrounds us with His presence. The only side left open is up! There are times, even at the age I am now, that I realize I am still growing. I'm not "there" yet. I need a safe place open only toward heaven where I can put down roots, grow, and develop into all that God created me to be.

God's frame around your life is both personal and time-sensitive. He knows that in some seasons you need a box-like frame in which to be protected, nourished, and given room to become the masterpiece He is growing you to be. *He alone is my safe place; his wraparound presence always protects me. For he is my champion defender* (Ps 62:2 TPT).

In other seasons, when it feels like your world is exploding or the attacks are coming from every side, you will need the protection of the wrap-around frame that holds you together. Your internal frame will shape your identity from the inside out.

Remember, in those "living-in-the-real-world-moments," the picture of who you are can't be altered by outside forces, only by the Master.

> *Wrapping himself around me like a shield, he is so generous with his gifts of grace and glory* (Ps 84:11 <u>TPT</u>).

You are framed. You are wrapped up in his "gifts of glory and grace." The one who framed you frames you!

My memories from today's moments with the Master…

_____

_____

_____

Conversation with the Master…

> *Lord, thank You for framing me, for holding me together. You are the boundaries that protect me and the structure that supports me. Thank You for wrapping yourself around me like a shield. Today I will live framed by Your love, grace, and glory. I celebrate being framed by You!*

DAY 21
SHAPED BY THE MASTER

Yet, O Lord, You are our Father; we are the clay, and You our Potter. And we all are the work of Your hand. (Is 64:8 AMP)

I was once given some valuable advice. At the time, I was struggling in a painful season of change. My friend's advice was simple and direct: "Remember where you came from." It was a firm reminder that my circumstances that day did not define me and God's design for my life wasn't deflected by them.

You see, it's easy to get so lost in today that we forget to value our story…what made us who we are. The fact is, I am who I am today because of a lifetime of relationships. I had parents who loved me, teachers who impacted me, friends who affected me (for better or worse), pastors and youth pastors who trained and equipped me…so many relationships, so much influence.

But the most influential relationship of all is with the One Who made me. Who I am didn't begin at the point of my earliest memory. In fact, it didn't begin when I was born. *For you formed my inward parts; you knitted me together in my mother's womb. I praise you, for I am fearfully and wonderfully made* (Ps 139:13, 14 ESV).

The amazing truth is, I came from the hands of God as an expression of His heart. In the beginning, He carefully formed man from the clay and then breathed life into that creation. In that breath was His DNA and that same DNA is carried on in all of us, His creation, His children.

That image is almost too big for us to grasp. It's a long journey from creation to yesterday! But the Bible gives us some brilliant word pictures to help us understand where we came from and the lessons to be learned from our journey from then to now and from there to here.

Jeremiah faced a challenging season as a prophet in Israel. The circumstances were confusing, in fact overwhelming. But God taught him through an object lesson: He sent him to the potter's house for a personal message: *Then I went down to the potter's house, and there he was, making something at the wheel. And the vessel that he made of clay was marred in the hand of the potter; so he made it again into another vessel, as it seemed good to the potter to make. Then the word of the Lord came to me, saying: "O house of Israel, can I not do with you as this potter? As the clay is in the potter's hand, so are you in My hand"* (Je 18:3-6 NKJV).

Making a pot requires a process. And even when the right process is followed, some pots don't work out on the first try. Some people don't either. But mess-ups don't have to end up in the throwaway bin. God doesn't throw the clay away. He makes it over again.

First, the potter works out the air bubbles; he removes the impurities; he moistens the clay—all before it ever begins to be shaped on the wheel. My Father follows a creative process as well. He works out the pockets of self, carefully removes the impurities of sin, and moistens the clay with the water of the Holy Spirit making me pliable, workable in His hands. His creative plan has always been, and is still, to make me a masterpiece, a reflection not of my own value, but of His character.

What we, in our flesh, forget is that our value as a vessel created by the Master is not in how we look on the outside. It's not our beautiful shape, stunning colors, or striking details. What determines our worth is what is in us. He created us to carry in our hearts the message of His plan for man, His masterpiece creation. That message is the Gospel. Paul described it like this: *But we have this treasure in earthen vessels, that the excellence of the power may be of God and not of us* (2Co 4:7 NKJV).

In the time Paul wrote this, people would have been very familiar with the value and variety of clay vessels available. Some might have been for water, some for food, but others might have been used to store, money, jewels, or parchments. In fact, the valuable Dead Sea Scrolls were found hidden in clay jars—literally treasures in earthen vessels! You see the value isn't in the outward design or shape of the pot, but in what is contained within.

When I remember where I came from…that I am clay, shaped and designed for a purpose, through a process, by God Himself…my perspective on today and its issues changes. I pursue His plan and make His purpose my priority.

Be a pot shaped by the plan, the purpose, and the priorities of the Master.

My memories from today's moments with the Master…

_____

_____

_____

Conversation with the Master…

God, I choose today to be clay in Your hands, ready to be shaped and molded, and even reshaped and remolded. I believe I am designed for a purpose and that Your purpose requires a process. From this moment, Lord, Your plan, purpose, and process are my priority.

DAY 22

THE OLD CHIMNEY

When your children ask you, "What do these stones mean?" tell them… (Jos 4:6 NIV).

Car rides can be boring. When I travel, I tend to look for interesting distractions along the way. For years I have been distracted by a structure I see just off the interstate during our drive from Missouri to Oklahoma. It's just an old stone chimney…no house, no foundation, not a sign of any life…just an old chimney.

But it fuels my imagination and ignites my curiosity. What is its story? Every time we pass it, I wonder about the home it once warmed, the family who once gathered around it, the memories it holds. Was the house destroyed, leaving the chimney as a grave marker? Or did the occupants desert it, abandoning the house to decay and the chimney to stand as a reminder of what once was? There's so much to be learned from what we leave behind.

Even masterpieces need markers. We need to have points of reference in our life that remind us of the journey we have made, the process we have experienced, and the distance we have come. It is valuable to be reminded of our story. Generations will build on the heritage we leave behind. They will gather around our old chimney and wonder, "What do these stones mean?"

This is not a new idea. Stones of remembrance have been erected since ancient days. You can read the story of Jacob's stone marker in Genesis 28. He built in the place where he was too weary to continue running.

During the night he spent stretched out on the ground, his head resting on rocks, he dreamed...about a ladder, and angels, and a personal promise from God! His first response to his experience makes me laugh; instead of being comforted by God's presence and promise, he was panic-stricken. He cried out, *How dreadful is this place!* (Ge 28:17 KJV).

But morning brought perspective. He realized it was a place of worship, not panic. He used the rocks that formed his pillow in the darkness to create a pillar in the daylight. He named it Bethel, which means "place of God's presence." And he determined that, when he returned home, that pillar would be the foundation for "God's house." (verse 22) The stones were a reminder of his story, the story of the place where he first experienced God's presence. They were a solid symbol not of where he stopped, but where he began his journey with God.

It's good to look back to the beginning. It gives not only perspective, but a promise for what is ahead. You can depend on God. He never changes. What He has done for you in the past, He will do again. Look at your "old chimney." It is the symbol of your story. Remind yourself of its message. The route to the future may involve going back past that marker of what He did before and claiming the heritage it reveals and the promise it stands for. Go past your old chimney and smile, maybe even do a little victory dance, because you know you can build even bigger and better based on what you learned there.

Remember the story of Joshua? He was a builder—of a nation, yes, but of altars as well. As dramatic as it was when the Jordan River rolled back and thousands of people walked through on dry ground, Joshua knew there were still obstacles to overcome in taking the land. God had a plan so that the people would never forget what happened at the beginning of their battles for the blessing. And so, at Gilgal, the site of Israel's first campout in the promised land, Joshua stacked up twelve stones that, according to God's instructions, had been carried from the middle of their miracle. They were to be a permanent reminder.

On that first day in Canaan, they all clearly remembered God's hand holding back the river and the dry path they used to cross over. But in years that followed there would be more battles to fight and obstacles to overcome. The altar provided a physical reminder of when the riverbed became a road to promise. It remained as a necessary marker for future generations. *This was so that everybody on earth would recognize how strong God's rescuing hand is and so that you would hold God in solemn reverence always* (Jos 4:24 MSG).

Your altar of remembrance may not be made of stones. And your story may not be about a ladder and angels; it may not be about the reversal of the laws of nature. A pile of stones may not be the method God uses for you. It's possible you won't recognize in the moment its value. But there will be a point where your path intersects with God's plan for your journey, and everything will be changed. Though it may appear ordinary in the moment, your place of remembrance will have extraordinary impact as you build it, share it, and return to it for encouragement and hope for the next step, the next miracle, the next "old chimney."

When someone asks, "what do these stones mean?" your past will speak to their present. You can share how going back takes you forward.

My memories from today's moments with the Master…

_____

_____

_____

Conversation with the Master…

> *Lord, today I want to build an altar of remembrance, a reminder of when my path intersected with Your plan and Your power was released. That will be my testimony; it will be the heritage I leave behind. In remembering what You have done, I claim Your power to continue the journey forward leaving landmarks of faith.*

DAY 23
MASTERPIECES IMAGINE

God can do anything, you know—far more than you could ever imagine or guess or request in your wildest dreams! (Ep 3:20 MSG).

I love listening to children play. Unlimited by fear, doubt, or impossibility, their conversations fly on the wings of imagination. Their minds create it, and it happens for them. The world becomes whatever they can make up. Invisible friends become best buddies; boxes turn into sports cars; and daydreams are daily events. A child can say, "Let's play like…" and what was only imagination becomes reality.

As I was writing this, I heard in my mind, "God is the ultimate imaginator." I couldn't remember hearing that word before, so I thought I was being imaginative myself and making up a new word. But not so much! I discovered that "imaginator" is a word—an in-the-dictionary kind of word! I checked. The definition is: "a person who creates (as an artistic or intellectual work)." ("imaginator"; *www.dictionary.com*) Clearly, God is himself the Divine Imaginator. He created the whole world that way!

I believe there is a deep connection between the Creator and children—maybe because we are most like our Father when we are imitating Him. As children, our lives are filled with seeds of imagination sown in our hearts by our Father, the Imaginator. They flourish there because our experience has not yet told us that creation is impossible, that we can't do the things in our heart. But, in fact, we are masterpieces with imagination. Sadly, the seeds of imagination in us die as they are uprooted by doubt and unbelief. Newsflash! Doubt doesn't come from God nor is it His nature. It is a dream killer. If your dreams of God's goodness are dying, to whom are you listening?

The fact is that Satan's plan is to substitute lust and evil thoughts for imagination and a pure mind. He does not want the seeds God has planted within us to grow and take root, so he plants substitute seeds. He tempts us to accept his cheap imitations for divine gifts. Imagination becomes lust, unholy desire. *For all that is in the world—the lust of the flesh, the lust of the eyes, and the pride of life—is not from the Father but is from the world* (1Jo 2:16 NKJV).

Since lust and pride are seeds that take root in the heart as substitutes for godly desires and imaginations, it's important that we be alert to their presence and weed them out. *Keep your heart with all diligence, for out of it spring the issues of life* (Pr 4:23 NKJV).

The word "issues" is also translated "boundaries." Therefore, we monitor what is growing in our heart by establishing boundaries beyond which any seeds—other than those God plants—aren't allowed to grow. What's in the heart is what determines our words, and our words determine what grows in our life. *The good person out of the good treasure of his heart produces good, and the evil person out of his evil treasure produces evil* (Lu 6:45 ESV).

Speaking of lust, evil, and boundaries seems to have taken us far from where we began with innocent children freely imagining. There is a huge divide between God's plan… *to achieve more than your greatest request, your most unbelievable dream, and exceed your wildest imagination* (Ep 3:20 TPT)…and the enemy's plan to destroy that destiny. Such forced separation can either discourage us and cause us to give up or it can inspire us to reclaim our dreams.

How? *We can demolish every deceptive fantasy that opposes God and break through every arrogant attitude that is raised up in defiance of the true knowledge of God. We capture, like prisoners of war, every thought and insist that it bow in obedience to the Anointed One* (2Co 10:5 TPT).

We can uproot deceptive fantasies. We can kill bad attitudes. We can win the battle for our imagination causing it to flourish and bring new life…just as our Father, the Imaginator does. We no longer "play like;" we "live like" the imaginative masterpiece God created us to be.

My memories from today's moments with the Master…

_____

_____

_____

Conversation with the Master…

*I am an imaginator, a child of **the** Imaginator!*

I want to imagine, dream, and create just like You do, Father! I am determined to reject every "deceptive fantasy" that opposes You and to guard my heart and mind, so that I produce "good treasure" from my heart of obedience.

DAY 24
MASTERPIECES INVEST WISELY

Take full advantage of every day as you spend your life for his purposes (Ep 5:16 TPT).

I read a story about a politically important and influential man who wrote on his planner one day, "Went fishing with my son today—a day wasted." His son also kept a journal. On that same day it read, "Went fishing with my father—the most wonderful day of my life!" The truth is, we decide whether to have wasted or wonderful days.

Most things in your life can be replaced. Days cannot. We don't have the opportunity to hit the delete button and start over; nor are we given the opportunity to reconsider and dig out of the trash what we've thrown away. I remember hearing a co-worker return from a meeting saying, "Well, that's two hours of my life I'll never get back!" And he was right. Two hours spent is not necessarily two hours invested. But a purpose fulfilled will move a day from wasted to wonderful.

So, how are your days going? Maybe the more important question—the one that moves you from spending to investing—is, do your days have purpose? The fact is the day will be spent. Whether you call it 24 hours, 1,440 minutes, or 86,400 seconds, it is time you will never get back. You decide: Will it be used or used up? Spent or invested?

Spending becomes investment when it is done for a purpose. Whether you're talking about money or about time, the same principle holds true. How much we have of either does not ultimately define its value. A million dollars may sound like a fortune, but carelessly or thoughtlessly spent, its value, in the end, is gone. One hundred dollars, on the other hand, sounds smaller in comparison, but invested wisely it can bring what financial planners call a great return on investment. That small amount can multiply in value. The difference is in using what we have for a purpose.

The questions we must ask ourselves are: In the end, what do I want to leave as my legacy? For what do I want people to remember me? And, most importantly for Christians, am I spending my days in ways that fulfill God's purposes for my life? These are pretty serious questions! Most of us feel as if we've aced the test if we manage to get from one day to the next without embarrassing ourselves, let alone fulfilling our God-given purpose. And so, we go slip sliding our way through days, months, even years, giving very little thought or effort to knowing God's plan and succeeding in achieving His purpose.

Remember, the Master's plan for his masterpiece doesn't change because it isn't completed in a day. *"For I know the plans I have for you"* declares the Lord, *"plans to prosper you and not harm you, plans to give you hope and a future"* (Je 29:11 NIV).

His plan gives you hope and takes you into the future. I'm so thankful He doesn't look at me on one of my no good, very bad days when I've accomplished little, and say, "No hope for her. No future, either. She didn't live up to my plan!"

Trust Him. He plans to complete the masterpiece that is you, the design He created before time began. He keeps shaping, touching up, and molding you day by day. Today you may not have taken full advantage of all the opportunities He had planned for you. But keep investing. Add as much as you can as often as you can for as long as you can. In the end, there will be an amazing return on investment.

I think that is what Paul, nearing the end of his life and having experienced all kinds of days, was trying to explain to Timothy…who was probably having some not-so-great-days of his own: *I have fought the good fight, I have finished the race, I have kept the faith. Now there is in store for me the crown of righteousness…* (2Ti 4:7, 8 NIV).

No doubt Paul had invested heavily in the purpose for which God had called him. The fact that he described it as a "fight" tells us that there were probably times when he didn't score a perfect 10 out of 10. It wasn't easy. There would have been no need for faith if it had been. The strength faith provided was a sort of dividend sharing program for the investment he was making.

Some days it's tempting to want that crown, that beautiful return on the investment, **now**. But, like Paul, we must follow the plan: Fight the fight. Finish the race. Fill up with faith as our source of strength and power.

Masterpieces continue to invest their days wisely even when they feel like failures or are tempted to quit. And each day, the Master continues to shape them into winners because they refuse to withdraw their investment before the race is complete and the crown of righteousness is theirs. You see, it isn't about the fight, it's about the finish.

Grab onto your days! Go for the gold! Get ready to wear that crown! That's God's plan!

My memories from today's moments with the Master…

_____

_____

_____

Conversation with the Master…

Lord, I declare that I will "take full advantage of every day," spending each one for Your purposes! I will invest my life for kingdom results rather than spending on temporary pleasure or comfort. I ask You for wisdom and clear direction as I live to fulfill Your purpose for my life. I choose from this day forward to invest in the kingdom rather than to spend on what cannot last.

DAY 25
YOU'RE A JEWEL!

When I gaze at your moon and your stars, mounted like jewels in their settings, I know you are the fascinating artist who fashioned it all (Ps 8:3 TPT).

This verse in Psalm 8 makes me think about David who wrote it. We call him King David. But long before he was a king, he was a young boy watching over his father's sheep; the only jewels he had were the ones he saw in the skies. The moon and stars were his introduction to the beauty and wonder of what God created. Later, as king of Israel, he possessed beautiful costly jewels in abundance…diamonds, sapphires, emeralds, rubies. The palace was full of them. But young boy or powerful king, he recognized the *"fascinating artist who fashioned it all."*

I remember a time when, as a little girl growing up in the mountains of Colorado, I was allowed to "sleep out" in the backyard. I got lost in the wonder of looking up at the stars. They appeared close enough to reach up and touch them. I saw them sparkle, almost like diamonds sprinkled across the velvety dark sky. I didn't know any scientific explanations of how they were formed or how long ago. I hadn't learned yet about constellations and orbits and how far away they truly were.

But I had listened in Bible classes. Like David, I knew God created the sun, the moon, and all those shimmering stars. And I believed He was a very good God to make something so beautiful. In the stillness of a summer night, I remember thinking God had done a great job on the sky. My appreciation was simple, but heartfelt. And I felt small and safe and secure.

All grown up now, I know more facts about stars and jewels. I've learned that diamonds are crystallized carbon, just one simple element, transformed by pressure and extreme heat deep in the earth. Pushed up by volcanic explosions, they are found in a limited number of places on the earth. They are rather unimpressive clear stones until they are taken to a lapidary who transforms a rock into a multifaceted jewel of great value. Like the diamond, all precious stones are transformed from their original form in the earth. God's chemistry converts common elements into priceless jewels.

Think about that! That is what God does…transforms simple things into something exquisite. I believe He wants us to understand that whether we **feel** like God's masterpiece or not is not the criteria He uses. He doesn't employ a sparkle meter to see if we are living up to His expectations and plans for us. During the pressure, the heat, the eruptions of reality, it's hard not to feel more like a rough stone than a beautiful gem. There is, however, a key word left out of that description: yet. We aren't perfectly faceted and polished gemstones **yet**.

So much of creation is a process. And if we try to rush past the formative stages, we will never become the finished masterpiece God sees. Every step brings us a little closer. But here's the great news: you are never **not** one of the Creator's precious, much-loved jewels. You may be in process, but in His eyes—more importantly in His heart—you are a perfectly formed, richly mounted, perfect diamond, shaped and perfected by the Master.

And God likes jewels! I am convinced this is true because you find them mentioned in His Word from Genesis to Revelation. They were in the Garden of Eden, and they are the building material of heaven. He even describes his people as jewels: *The Lord their God will save his people on that day as a shepherd saves his flock. They will sparkle in his land like jewels in a crown. How attractive and beautiful they will be* (Ze 9:16, 17 <u>NIV</u>).

You're a Jewel!

God doesn't play favorites. Rest assured, you are His child, and you will have your time to shine! From rough to redeemed, you are His jewel.

My memories from today's moments with the Master…

_____

_____

_____

Conversation with the Master…

God, like David, "I know You are the fascinating artist who fashioned it all." You transform what is ordinary into something beautiful and precious. Without You I am ordinary, but I put myself in Your hands to be changed from rough stone to sparkling, redeemed jewel.

DAY 26
MASTERPIECES DON'T NEED MASKS

> *But the Lord said to Samuel, 'Do not look at his appearance or at his physical stature, because I have refused him. For the Lord does not see as man sees* (1 Sa 16:7 <u>NKJV</u>).

Not gonna lie, very few people ever see me without make-up. I have a face I wear in public for others to see, and then there's the face behind the mask. I've been known to pretend I wasn't home when the doorbell rang because my face was bare and I hadn't combed my hair…face bare, messy hair, I'm not there!

I know at a deeper level that most people would never notice my unimproved appearance; if they did, it would probably comfort them that someone else looks that bad, too. But let's be honest here, it's not about making everyone else happy. It's about hiding what doesn't make me happy.

Not every mask is make-up. Some masks are the smile we paste on to make people think we are "doing fine" when we're not truly fine at all. It's a much more comfortable response to "How are you?" than the truth: I'm exhausted…can't sleep at night…feel as if I can't keep going much longer." Another commonly worn mask is busy-ness. It's a mask of constant motion…movement intended to look impressive while warding off uncomfortable personal conversations or relationships.

What masks do you wear? Is there a style you wear so that you fit in where you feel you can't otherwise? Are there places you go and activities you are a part of that you don't enjoy, but feel it's expected? It's just "what we do?" It's the mask we wear. Maybe you try to hide all the scars and

Masterpiece

bruises that reveal the life you have lived. What would everyone think if you didn't?

The truth? Who you are is much more than your mask. And what you have experienced is much more than something to hide. It is a testimony to the fact that you are who you are…and you are a masterpiece.

I recently read an interview with an actress who has been known for her beauty and talent. She was asked why, unlike many people her age and in her profession, she hadn't had plastic surgery. Her response was thought-provoking. She wants to keep the wrinkles in her forehead as a sign of her amazement at the beauty of life. The ones around her mouth speak of how much she laughed and how much she kissed. She even wants to keep the black circles under her eyes, because they are the outward sign of her hidden memories of sadness and tears. They are part of her. She loves their beautiful message. They are the true indicators of her many life experiences.

Every face tells a story. It may not yet be the story written by God Himself from His viewpoint, but it will be. *Your eyes saw my unformed body; all the days ordained for me were written in your book before one of them came to be"* (Ps 139:16 TPT).

God saw us before we got our make-up on, straightened our masks, and became great pretenders. He can't be fooled by plastic surgery, or by any other attempt to "fix" the masterpiece He created. It's not that those things are wrong or sinful. They are unnecessary to our goal of becoming a masterpiece. You have nothing to hide. Our theme verse today finishes with the words, *for man looks at the outward appearance, but the Lord looks at the heart* (1Sa 16:7 NKJV).

Instead of his hunky brothers, David—the little brother who was out herding sheep and totally overlooked when the inspection was being made—was chosen by God to be king. The day Samuel anointed David to serve he was a rosy-cheeked boy in a shepherd's robe. He wasn't tall. He wasn't impressive. Even he probably didn't realize the qualities he had that prepared him to lead God's people. But God did.

In the book God has written for your life and mine there are stories we haven't experienced and probably would never imagine for ourselves. We probably wouldn't believe they were possible if we heard about them. Long after David was anointed to be king, he was still amazed at how God saw him. He wondered in Psalm 8, *Why would you bother with puny, mortal man or care about human beings? Yet what honor you have given to men, created only a little lower than Elohim, crowned with glory and magnificence. You have delegated to them rulership over all you have made, with everything under their authority, placing earth itself under the feet of your image-bearers* (Ps 8:4-6 TPT).

That answers every question about your qualifications to go mask-free. You are God's "image bearer." You wear a crown of glory and magnificence. You rule with authority.

No mask required! You don't cover up a masterpiece.

My memories from today's moments with the Master…

_____

_____

_____

Conversation with the Master…

> *God, I know I need to take off my masks. Because I know I can trust You, I choose to see myself as You do and to find my identity in bearing Your image—not in listening to the world's opinions or giving in to self-criticism. I don't need a mask! I am Your masterpiece!*

DAY 27

YOU WANT ME TO DO WHAT?

So he, trembling and astonished, said, "Lord, what do You want me to do?" Then the Lord said to him, "Arise and go into the city, and you will be told what you must do" (Ac 9:6 NKJV).

I may have a strange sense of humor. When I read the story about Saul meeting up with Jesus on the road to Damascus, I laugh. This story plays out in my head as very funny. I can imagine Saul, all full of himself, riding along with his head high and a smug smile on his face. Then, inexplicably, he finds himself rolling around in the dirt, pride out the door! The men with him could hear Jesus' voice but could not see Him, so it must have been at least a little amusing to watch the big, (self-)important man not only rolling on the ground but talking to himself.

In my imagination, this is a funny scene. It's the moment when the sanctimonious met the Savior. But, after the fall off his horse and a roll in the dirt, followed by conversation with an invisible person, he said something I believe was very out of character. Notice what he asked: *Lord, what do you want me to do?* The guy who was accustomed to giving orders was asking for them…from someone no one else in the group could see. And the answer was: *Arise, go into the city, and you will be told what you must do.*

Saul struck fear into the hearts of Christians everywhere. He was the one who had watched Stephen's stoning—maybe on orders he himself gave—and now he was being told to get up, go into the city where he had planned to take charge, and humbly wait for someone to tell him what to do next. Talk about role reversal!

My laughter about the story isn't about Saul's suffering. I'm not that cruel! It is about the way in which, when Jesus shows up, things are generally turned upside down and inside out. Moments before Saul hit the dust, he would never have considered taking orders from the One he hated. He was ordinarily obeyed rather than obedient. But his whole life changed in an instant. Before, he would have responded, "You want me to do what?!" Now he simply obeyed.

Don't be surprised if you experience a you-want-me-to-do-what moment. The Gospel is all about reversals. A relationship with Christ begins with a complete turnaround and leads to a life of opposites.

Therefore, if anyone is in Christ, he is a new creation; old things have passed away; behold all things have become new (2Co 5:17 NKJV).

The old dies and what replaces it is not simply a remake of the old, but a new creation. The flesh does not understand nor approve the new version; it may ask, "You want me to do what?!" It's uncomfortable with this new life.

One of the mistakes Christians make is assuming that being a Christian means there will be no more problems and only smooth sailing ahead. They assume that if a situation is painful or in any way difficult it isn't God's will. In fact, Satan is blamed for a lot of things that are in reality the result of Christians' bad choices. We should not be surprised when discomfort, trouble, pain, and persecution—the bad stuff—happen to Christians. Jesus told His disciples, *In the world you will have tribulation; but take courage, I have overcome the world* (Jn 16:33 NASB). The difference is our response: take courage. (Some versions have "take heart." Others say "cheer up!" None say "whine" or "give up.") We choose the effect we allow in our life.

Paul explained (years after he met Jesus on the dusty Damascus road and was given a new name and a new life), *Yes, and all who desire to live godly in Christ Jesus will suffer persecution"* (2Ti 3:12 NKJV).

He told the Corinthian church, *"We are hard pressed on every side, but not crushed; perplexed, but not in despair; persecuted, but not abandoned; struck down, but not destroyed. Though outwardly we are wasting away, yet inwardly we are being renewed day by day"* (2Co 4:8, 9, 16 NKJV).

Being made new is a process. It isn't completed instantaneously. It would be so great if once we were saved, we never suffered or struggled ever again! That is not our promise nor our experience.

The "what" He wants us to do is have a new response to old problems, to allow a major attitude readjustment. We can't always change our circumstances. But we can change how we deal with them. Jesus instructed us to be courageous and to live in the truth that He has already fought and won the battle for us. Paul cautions us to prioritize living godly lives over living comfortable lives. He gave the key to that to the Corinthians: be renewed day by day.

Undoubtedly, we would all prefer a one and done deal on this suffering issue. The truth is Jesus died for our sin once and for all. However, forgiven doesn't mean consequence-free. The victory over those consequences lies in believing what Jesus, not our circumstance, says, being spiritually renewed day by day, and obeying. Remember, no matter what you face, Christ has promised that we always win. Paul told the church at Corinth, *But we thank God for giving us the victory as conquerors through our Lord Jesus, the Anointed One* (1Co 15:57 TPT).

We win! See you in the winner's circle!

My memories from today's moments with the Master…

_____

_____

_____

Conversation with the Master...

*Lord, when Saul fell on the road, blind and confused, he asked You what to do; You answered and put him back on the road—this time to victory. I believe You have made me a new creation and will continue to renew me day by day as I walk my new road with a new attitude of victory. I **am** a conqueror through Jesus!*

DAY 28

TIME...NOT GOD'S PROBLEM

But do not forget this one thing, dear friends: With the Lord a day is like a thousand years, and a thousand years are like a day. The Lord is not slow in keeping his promise, as some understand slowness. Instead, he is patient with you... (2Pe 3:8-9 NIV).

God is a now God. At first glance it appears that would mean He does everything right now, this minute. But that assessment comes from our human viewpoint. God's now has little to do with time and everything to do with eternity. He is not regulated by clocks and calendars. In fact, time is our problem, not His. He operates outside of its control and influence.

So what does that mean for us in our relationship with Him? For one thing, it means that even when we feel as if we are waiting forevvvverrrrrr, He feels no pressure to adjust to a schedule He never authorized. The truth that a thousand years is like a day to Him debunks the illusion that we can impose our deadlines on Him. He keeps His promises, not our schedules. When it comes to the good things He has promised us, we are more than willing to opt for the day over the thousand years. But how do we respond when our wait feels less like days and more like a thousand years?

Patience. The right answer is to be patient. No masterpiece is produced and perfected without a process; and a process operating **in** time **requires** time. Every mother can understand this. We live in a world where new lives require a nine-month process.

Masterpiece

I will never forget the thrill I experienced the first time I heard that I was pregnant…there was a masterpiece on the way! But delivering that little masterpiece into the world was a process. Some, actually many, of the experiences along the way required patience. It was uncomfortable feeling and seeing my body grow and change. I remember standing in front of a mirror and wondering if my body could ever look "normal" again. I gagged every time I brushed my teeth. And seeing raw meat was nauseating to me on an unprecedented level. I would never want to be critical of God, but I really questioned His wisdom in establishing this 40-week schedule for birthing that child!

I knew God had a plan; I believed in Him and His plan. Yet, I admit, sometimes I whined about the wait time in the process. Despite all my impatience, when it was time…when the child had been nourished and developed according to the Master's schedule…she was born. She arrived ten days late, was breech, and was delivered by cesarean. But to me, she was perfect as promised.

In what I believe is another sign of God's goodness, I am no longer in the child-birthing season of my life. But I am still moving forward in claiming the promises for my life as God's masterpiece. I am learning lessons about living for the eternal God…now.

I am learning not to judge my circumstances too soon, but to know if I'm not satisfied with my **now** it's because He's not finished with my **forever.**

I am learning faith allows me to "call into being things that don't even exist yet" (Ro 4:17 TPT). I have a promise that "not now" is not necessarily "never." I can claim promises unfulfilled…yet.

I am learning faith moves me forward when feelings, due to my own impatience, would cause me to forfeit incredible promises.

I am learning that Psalm 30:5 (NKJV) is true: *Weeping may endure for a night, but joy comes in the morning.* God's promises are as real in the tearful night as in the joyful morning.

I am learning that it is true: Time is my problem not God's.

My memories from today's moments with the Master…

_____

_____

_____

Conversation with the Master…

> *Lord, help me to remember when I'm tempted to be impatient that You are not bound by my schedule…I'm Your masterpiece in process and You don't consult a watch or check a calendar. Help me to be patient and to remember that "not yet" is not "never." I willingly claim Your promises by faith, calling "those things which are not as though they were."*

DAY 29

A WALK WITH THE MASTER

And what does the Lord require of you but to do justly, to love mercy, and to walk humbly with your God? (Mi 6:8 <u>NKJV</u>)

It may sound dramatic or overly romantic, but every time my husband takes my hand, wherever we are, I fall in love all over again. It's a simple reminder of the connection we have. Without a word, he tells me, "I'm here beside you. I'm protecting you. You're mine, and I'm holding on to you. I love you." I would know all those things if he weren't holding my hand, weren't walking beside me, but in those moments when we are linked together, I love receiving his message.

I know his hands, their touch, their appearance, the scars and the callouses. Everything about them reminds me of his story…of the time he caught his right hand in a cement mixer…of when his cousin told him to hold the wood while he used the hatchet and Denver's finger was sliced nearly off…of the hours he spent strumming strings and learning chords to develop into a wonderful guitarist. Those hands. I know so much from his hands.

Before Denver came into my life, I did not have someone with whom to walk, share my life, and talk. It was a season in which I learned to walk and talk with God, to stay so close to Him I could hear His voice, hold His hand, and feel His touch. My relationship with Him was changed forever as I learned to allow Him to be my husband.

The root meaning for the word translated as "walk" in the Bible is "continually be conversant." That means, according to <u>Oxford Languages,</u> "to be familiar with or knowledgeable about something." It's easy to understand that God wants us to walk with Him. He wants us to learn to know Him, to be familiar with His ways…to be conversant with Him.

Do you realize that God wants nothing **from** you? He wants **you**. So many times, when we want a relationship with someone, we try to grab their attention; we change ourselves to please them; we attempt to earn their love. God's requirements are nothing like that. Reread the key verse for today: *What does the Lord require of you but to do justly, to love mercy, and to walk humbly with your God"* (Mi 6:8 NKJV)?

In the verses leading up to this one, other options are offered such as bowing down before Him, bringing burnt offerings, offering rivers of oil, even offering one's firstborn. None of that was what God was looking for. His plan is uncomplicated: live a just life, shaped by mercy, and walked out right beside Him. We make it difficult. He doesn't.

From the beginning it was God's intent that man, His creative masterpiece, walk with Him. Sin messed that up in Eden. Apparently, prior to that, the usual plan was for an evening stroll through the garden, just God, Adam, and Eve. Notice what it says in Genesis 3:8: *And they heard the sound of the Lord God walking in the garden in the cool of the day, and Adam and his wife hid themselves from the presence of the Lord God among the trees of the garden" (NKJV).*

They resorted to hiding rather than walking. God knew exactly where they were and what they had done, but He gave them an opportunity to come clean and maybe even continue to walk with Him. That didn't happen. Even today people miss out on the walk they could enjoy with their Creator because they are trying to cover up for their sin.

Can you imagine walking side-by-side with God…talking, learning, even laughing and enjoying life together? It's not impossible. A few Bible chapters after the story of Adam and Eve, one of their descendants resumed the walking-with-God-plan: *So all the days of Enoch were three hundred and sixty-five years. And Enoch walked with God; and he was not, for God took him"* (Ge 5: 23-24 NKJV).

Amazing! He walked out of time and into eternity with God—simply because he walked with God!

His plan is still for us to "walk humbly with our God." You may feel as if you've tried everything, and every attempt has been a failure; all you want to do is hide. God's preference is not a spiritual game of hide-and-seek. His plan is to walk with us, to hold our hand...to allow us to become "conversant" with Him.

It will be in those moments of walking hand in hand with Him that you will become familiar with your Master. You will come to know Him personally and well. And whatever happens before or after your focused fitness time with Him, your life will be different. Time with the Master allows Him to perfect His masterpiece...a creation that reflects His character, His nature, and His love.

Today, walk with God. Become conversant with Him. It will be well worth the effort. Need some encouragement? Remember Paul's words in Ephesians 2:10: *For we are his workmanship, created in Christ Jesus for good works, which God prepared beforehand that we should walk in them* (NKJV)

You were created to walk!

My memories from today's moments with the Master...

_____

_____

_____

Conversation with the Master...

> *Father, how amazing that You desire to walk with me! Your presence is the promise of Your plan. So, as You continue shaping me into the masterpiece You planned and designed me to be, I want to become "conversant" with You...to know and take on Your character, Your nature, Your love. As we walk together, make this masterpiece more and more like You, Master.*

DAY 30
COME LINGER LONGER

For from days of old no one has heard, nor has ear perceived, nor has the eye seen a God besides You, who works and acts in behalf of the one who [gladly] waits for him (Is 64:4 AMP)

My husband and I both enjoy perfumes. We can spend an inordinate amount of time in the perfume outlet store sniffing and "trying on" a ridiculous number of fragrances. Just any option won't do. He says he searches for one for me that says, "Come hither, linger longer." I feel the same way when selecting one for him! We enjoy the fragrance, but we value the lingering result. It's great for our relationship!

Do you find yourself rushing in and out of God's presence? Or do you linger longer? Here's a relationship hint: God really likes it when you wait in His presence. Your relationship with Him will take on depth and intimacy as you give Him your time, your full attention, and your presence.

You can see how time spent with Jesus makes a difference in a story told by Luke that involved walking, two men, and a lingering experience with Jesus. Their conversation during the seven-mile journey from Jerusalem to Emmaus was sober, almost hopeless. Jesus joined them as they walked, but they didn't recognize they were with the One for whom they were grieving. You would think the conversation with Him would have revealed His identity. But no! It was not until they invited Him to linger longer with them and share a meal that they knew Him. *Then their eyes were opened and they recognized him, and he disappeared from their sight. They asked each other, "Were not our hearts burning within us while he talked with us on the road and opened the Scriptures to us"* (Lu 24:31-32 NIV)?

It is in the commitment of waiting, the intimacy of lingering, that identity is revealed.

Daily life in our world doesn't encourage lingering. If traffic slows very much, we're tempted to take the closest exit and find a faster route. If a better or more exciting option is presented, we dive into that distraction. We create and live by to-do lists while never creating a to-be list. We live in a rushing, hurrying, scrambling world.

God, however, calls us to waiting, staying, remaining, persisting… lingering with Him. While we are being pressured to create and follow agendas, God is calling us to walk with Him, to measure our steps by His, and to become more like Him, because He **is** our agenda rather than **on** it.

Lingering ruins agendas but builds relationship.

You have permission to linger.

You have permission to be… even if you don't complete your to-do list.

It is not God's plan or desire for us to have a drive-through relationship with Him. Running through to pick up a quick snack of His Word will never satisfy. Relationship requires waiting. Go to the high-end restaurant of living in His presence. He offers a massive menu. As you linger over your meal you will have time to savor its flavor, appreciate its richness, and draw nourishment from its variety. God enjoys the time you linger with Him. You need it. He uses it for your good.

One of my favorite Bible stories is about the lame man who begged at the Gate Beautiful where people passed by as they entered the temple. He was used to quick glances and maybe a small gift. But then He met Peter and John who had experience with spending time with Jesus and being changed by it.

The story in Acts 3 says the man saw the two disciples going into the temple. Everyone else kept going, but they lingered. In the lingering was revelation. They recognized that the beggar needed more than money. He expected nothing else. Instead, Peter gave Him relationship with Jesus. Speaking Jesus' name brought more than money; it released healing and a new life. Peter said, *"[begin now to] walk and go on walking"* (Ac 3:6 AMP)! When he was lifted to his feet he was lifted out of his past and into God's presence. And it completely changed him! He was free to walk with his Healer. *He went into the temple with them, walking and leaping and praising God"* (Ac 3:8 AMP).

Exposure to God's presence draws us to linger there. The man once lame was leaping. Pretty sure that was not what people in the temple were accustomed to seeing. I'm also sure more lives were changed that day than that of the leaping lame man.

Sometimes lingering isn't a matter of time, but of focus. As the man shifted his focus and looked into Peter's eyes, he was introduced to the only One who could give him what he needed rather than what he had on his agenda. The first steps he took in his walk with Jesus were running, leaping, and praising God. I like that! He had been waiting for money, but now he had a brand-new life.

God has amazing things to pour out on us when we wait for Him. No one else, no other god, has ever been heard of or seen who works on behalf of the one who lingers with Him.

Maybe, just maybe, if you linger with Him, you will be a running, leaping, praising masterpiece, too.

My memories from today's moments with the Master...

_____

_____

_____

Conversation with the Master...

> *I want to linger longer with You today, Master. I want to take time to experience Your presence. I believe that if I set aside my agenda and open my heart to You, the fragrance of Your Spirit will permeate my life. Here I am, Lord, lingering with You.*

DAY 31

WRAPPED UP

Because I set you, Yahweh, always close to me, my confidence will never be weakened, for I experience your wraparound presence every moment (Ps 16:8 TPT).

There is a rather mysterious process that happens when we spend a lot of time with someone. That person's character and characteristics become part of us. It is not a replacement process, but rather a melding together. The two become a blend of both. I have seen this happen in my life. Sometimes it is a casual, maybe temporary, process; other times it becomes more intrinsic to my identity.

For example, when I was in my teens, we moved around to different parts of the country. I tended to absorb the different accents and expressions of the region in which I lived. I easily picked up the colloquial idioms they used. I said "you guys" when I was in the North and West and y'all in the South (just couldn't do you'ns in the Ozarks!). I didn't plan the change, didn't initially even notice the shift from one to the other. I simply took on that with which I was surrounded.

Being married to Denver has been a melding, blending, subtle, and not-so-subtle process of change, too. Over time, consciously and unconsciously, we have absorbed one another's influence. I tell more corny jokes now. He catches himself, like me, compulsively wiping the faucet, sink and counter whenever he washes his hands. But it goes deeper. I have begun to live by faith in ways I never did before…because he has taught me by his daily living patterns. In return, he has learned that patience isn't punishment and waiting has rewards…because that is my pattern.

Because we share space, physically, emotionally, and spiritually, and we value that connection, we continually meld our lives into one. As a result of this new blend, we are both better than we could be separately. In ways in which even we are probably not entirely aware, we become more like one another.

That is the relationship the Master offers us as His masterpieces. His presence is our identity, our safe place, our security. *He alone is my safe place; his wraparound presence always protects me. For he is my champion defender; there's no risk of failure with God! So why would I let worry paralyze me, even when troubles multiply around me* (Ps 62:2 TPT)?

Our masterpiece identity is never threatened, but instead, it is defined more clearly when we remain in His presence. We keep Him close. We put our confidence in Him. In response, His love, His strength, and His presence become part of us. We can become so completely wrapped up in Him that He and His qualities are what people see when they see us. Even better, when we are tempted to doubt, to fear, or to rely on the resources we bring to the situation, we can shift the focus to the One in whom we are wrapped: the Master.

Only in the environment of the Master is the identity of the masterpiece fully revealed. You will only become your best self and live your best life when you live in His presence, draw from His nature, and rely on His creative skill. He is covering you! He has your back; He stands beside you; He has gone before you. In His presence you are what He sees you to be.

It's time to claim all the benefits of being God's creative masterpiece!

> *Because you are close to me and always available, my confidence will never be shaken, for I experience your wraparound presence every moment* (Ps 16:8 TPT).

> *You empower me for victory with your wrap-around presence. Your power within makes me strong to subdue, and by*

stooping down in gentleness you strengthened me and made me great" (Ps 18:35 TPT)!

You're my place of quiet retreat, and your wrap-around presence becomes my shield as I wrap myself in your word (Ps 119:114 TPT).

Imagine! If just a moment in the presence of the Master can make you a new person, what will living there do?

Relationship is a choice, even with God. You can choose to be wrapped up in His presence—or not. He already chose to love you, already made you a masterpiece…always has loved you, always will!

In the days when I drove my daughters to school and dropped them off, we had a routine. As they jumped out of the car, I would call out, "Always remember. Never forget. Your mama loves you!"

Your Father has the same message for His masterpieces: Always remember. Never forget. Your Father loves you! Start and live each day all wrapped up in His love.

Always remember. Never Forget!

My memories from today's moments with the Master…

_____

_____

_____

Conversation with the Master…

You, God, are my safe place. Your presence wraps me up in love. Your Word brings me strength and confidence for every situation. Today I have access to all I need as I remain behind the shield of Your presence and draw power from Your Word.

CITATIONS

Bible versions cited:
New King James Version
New Living Translation
King James Version
Amplified Version
Amplified Classic Version
New International Version
The Message
New American Standard Bible
English Standard Version

Dictionaries cited:
www.dictionary. Com

Printed in the USA
CPSIA information can be obtained
at www.ICGtesting.com
LVHW040847230824
789041LV00001B/65